MW00653722

ıE CONSTITUTION OF IMPERIUM

RONNIE D. LIPSCHUTZ

THE CONSTITUTION
OF IMPERIUM

Paradigm Publishers

Boulder • London

All rights reserved. No part of the publication may be transmitted or reproduced in any media or form, including electronic, mechanical, photocopy, recording, or informational storage and retrieval systems, without the express written consent of the publisher.

Copyright © 2009 Paradigm Publishers

Published in the United States by Paradigm Publishers, 3360 Mitchell Lane, Suite E, Boulder, CO 80305 USA.

Paradigm Publishers is the trade name of Birkenkamp & Company, LLC, Dean Birkenkamp, President and Publisher.

Library of Congress Cataloging-in-Publication Data

Lipschutz, Ronnie D.
The constitution of imperium / Ronnie D. Lipschutz.
    p. cm.
  Includes bibliographical references and index.
ISBN 13: 978-1-59451-576-7 (hardcover : alk paper)
    1. United States—Foreign relations—2001. 2. International organization. 3. Globalization. 4. International economic relations. 5. World politics—21st century. I. Title.

JZ1480.L57 2008
327.73—dc22

                                    2008018108

Printed and bound in the United States of America on acid-free paper that meets the standards of the American National Standard for Permanence of Paper for Printed Library Materials.

Designed and typeset by Cheryl Hoffman.

13 12 11 10 09   1 2 3 4 5

Imperium: Command; absolute power; supreme or imperial power[1]

—*Oxford English Dictionary On-line*

The great struggles of the twentieth century between liberty and totalitarianism ended with a decisive victory for the forces of freedom—and a single sustainable model for national success: freedom, democracy, and free enterprise. In the twenty-first century, only nations that share a commitment to protecting basic human rights and guaranteeing political and economic freedom will be able to unleash the potential of their people and assure their future prosperity. People everywhere want to be able to speak freely; choose who will govern them; worship as they please; educate their children—male and female; own property; and enjoy the benefits of their labor. These values of freedom are right and true for every person, in every society—and the duty of protecting these values against their enemies is the common calling of freedom-loving people across the globe and across the ages.

—George W. Bush, *The National Security Strategy of the United States,* September 2002

Championing freedom advances our interests because the survival of liberty at home increasingly depends on the success of liberty abroad. Governments that honor their citizens' dignity and desire for freedom tend to uphold responsible conduct toward other nations, while governments that brutalize their people also threaten the peace and stability of other nations. Because democracies are the most responsible members of the international system, promoting democracy is the most effective long-term measure for strengthening international stability; reducing regional conflicts; countering terrorism and terror-supporting extremism; and extending peace and prosperity. To protect our Nation and honor our values, the United States seeks to extend freedom across the globe by leading an international effort to end tyranny and to promote effective democracy.

—*The National Security Strategy of the United States,* March 2006, Sec. II.C.

CONTENTS

Acknowledgments

This book began to take form—as did many others—following the events of September 11, 2001. The text was not committed to paper (or, rather, computer) until the summer of 2006, and the version you are reading was last revisited in March 2008. With the end of George W. Bush's presidency in sight, this might seem a rather late date to publish a volume on empire. Yet there are excellent reasons to think that many of the legal and practical innovations of the Bush administration's various arms and agencies will not go away with a new president or Congress. Indeed, the structural problems that gave rise to 9/11 and similar incidents developed long before that fateful day and will remain to taunt and haunt the United States for a long time. Some may doubt this, or hope for better times; I do not.

Although all that is written here is my responsibility, I owe a great deal to colleagues, critics, and interlocutors. They include, in no particular order, Sandra Halperin, Mary Ann Tétreault, Kees van der Pijl, Ronen Palan, Phil Cerny, Paul Lubeck, Shelley Hurt, and Ben Lozano, among many others. I owe special thanks to Alexander Reed-Krase, who doggedly read and questioned every chapter of the first draft, and to Jennifer Knerr, whose encouragement was instrumental to its completion. And, of course, I owe undying love and gratitude to Mary Wieland, who has stuck with me through thick, thin, and in between.

Chapter One

Constitution

Since September 11, 2001, the Bush administration and its counsels in the U.S. Department of Justice have been devising a Constitution of Imperium.[1] Whether, in the long run, this project will succeed on its own terms—laying the legal foundations for a global Imperium—is not yet clear.[2] Nonetheless, an imperial constitution is being written, and an Imperium is being constituted. Neither will be easy to undo once inscribed and imposed on the world. This is not, strictly speaking, a new project: Both the constitution and Imperium have been in the making for many decades, albeit not with any clear intentionality—initiated in the aftermath of World War II and gradually expanded over the following decades. It is only since 2001, however, that its shape and contents have started to become clear. The Constitution of Imperium—which should not be confused with the U.S. Constitution—has been doing work in the "nonsovereign" spaces of Guantanamo Bay, Cuba, Abu Ghraib, Baghdad, and CIA black detention sites around the world, among others, whose prisoners, in the words of George W. Bush, "represent no nation." The operation of the Constitution of Imperium is visible, so to speak, in the National Security Agency's (NSA) surveillance and data-mining of electronic communications between the United States and the rest of the world (the latter having no standing in American courts or under American law), in the rules and practices required of foreign others by various U.S. government agencies, and in the myriad of other regulatory and legal demands made by the United States of both its citizens and those living in and traveling among other countries. The contradictions of Imperium are apparent in international politics but are most evident in struggles among the White House, Congress, and courts over the extent and prerogatives of executive authority—the "sole organ"—as codified in the U.S. Constitution, the constraints of which have been tested and substantially rejected by the president, vice president, and advisers throughout the executive branch.[3]

The paradox here—if, indeed, there is one—is that, in testing these limits, the Bush administration has sought to constitute an "imperial authority" that, by its own definition, would be nowhere subject to the long-assumed checks of either the U.S. Constitution, Congress, and the courts or international law. Instead, this authority operates outside the boundaries of American sovereignty, in defiance of the so-called international community and the United Nations, and in violation of the law of nations. Indeed, it is more accurate to say that the Constitution of Imperium is being written under the terms of normalizing what Carl Schmitt called "the state of exception." This is a situation in which—legal and constitutional statutes offering no clear direction or guidance to a state or its leaders when confronting a national emergency—a self-constituted authority might be driven to act in an extraconstitutional fashion. Not even on September 11, 2001, was it wholly evident that such a condition existed—but then, states of exception are constructed by those who take it upon themselves to make such judgments. In *Political Theology,* Schmitt proffered the now well-worn phrase "sovereign is he who decides the exception." Specifying the exception permits the decider to act above and abrogate such law as there might be and make legal whatever he or she might decide to do. Whether the events of that fateful day did constitute an "exception" in the Schmittian sense is a point of debate (and I shall argue in this book that it was not); that the Bush administration treated it as an exception meriting—no, demanding—extraconstitutional behavior, cannot be denied.[4]

We should not, however, imagine that, on September 12, 2001, Justice Department lawyers set out to craft a Constitution of Imperium, nor should we think that this project was launched at the express order of the White House or some other center of legal authority. To be sure, the president's and vice president's counselors began immediately to think about the legal and juridical bases for retaliation and revenge against those believed responsible for the 9/11 atrocities. As it became evident that those parties were associated with a "nonstate" network based in a country whose sovereignty and cohesion were being contested, the lawyers in the Department of Justice also began to argue that the international "laws of war" codified in the Geneva Conventions and other treaties did not provide sufficient legal cover for the military actions required to pursue and capture or kill those malefactors. Indeed, those laws acted as obstructions to sovereign action. Once President Bush declared a global war on terror (GWOT), it was deemed necessary to formulate a legal basis for actions and policies that might be required in prosecuting this and subsequent wars. Such seems to have been the general sentiment, given the possibility that any legal rationalization based wholly on the U.S. Constitution and the Geneva Conventions might be challenged in and overturned by American courts. Thus, the lawyers went to work crafting a constitutional framework that the courts and Congress could not touch.[5]

In doing this work, those lawyers—the most notorious of whom are probably David Addington, Vice President Dick Cheney's right-hand man, and John Yoo, currently a professor of law at the University of California–Berkeley's Boalt Hall—laid the foundation for a legal order that transcends and, indeed, overawes international law and its notional embeddedness in the sovereign states that are that law's subjects. We ought to ask, of course, why a state of exception requires *any* law or legal justification at all, especially if the sovereign decider wields the military force thought necessary to impose the state's will on all others. Such a question disregards, on the one hand, that the legitimacy of law and its associated actions rest on general acceptance by those who are its subjects. It also elides, on the other hand, what seems to be lawyers' obsessive need to reproduce their profession by formulating the legal reasoning underpinning any action that might be construed as an "exception," thereby bringing it within the law. There is no reason, either, that a Constitution of Imperium need be presented to its "subjects" for ratification, or even that it materialize as a text to be kept under glass and reprinted in schoolbooks. After all, the United Kingdom has no *written* constitution, even though it possesses a constitutional order resulting from almost one thousand years of royal decrees, parliamentary sovereignty, and legal jurisprudence. And from whom would ratification be asked? To offer such a constitution for approval by its subjects would immediately impose limits on sovereignty, which is precisely what the new legal order is intended to circumvent.[6]

This is a book about these odd and somewhat inexplicable actions and events, and about the Constitution of Imperium and the constitution of imperium: how the American empire has been constituted, especially since 1945, in terms of laws, practices, structures, mentalities, and materiality, and how emergent legal reasoning and practice have been laying the philosophical and physical basis for this empire's global authority. In this book I do not write about other empires in history, or whether the American empire is similar to or different from them. I do not argue here whether this Imperium is good or evil or if it has been acquired in a fit of absentmindedness or hegemonic behavior and benevolence.[7]

I do try to show how, historically, materially, and genealogically, this Imperium has been constructed since the attacks of September 11, 2001, and how it was immanent in the policies and practices pursued by the United States between August 13, 1945, and September 10, 2001. Imperium was by no means inevitable or determined at the end of World War II or the Cold War or during the "post–Cold War" era of the 1990s. Nor, despite the overwhelming military power and considerable global economic and structural capacities of the United States today, should Imperium somehow be seen as a "natural" consequence of the need for defense of the homeland and America's global interests. Rather, it is best understood as the outcome of decisions and actions often made in an ad hoc and opportunistic fashion to address specific needs and fears, along Weber's "tracks of ideals and interests," but without a clear view of where action might lead, producing long-term historical results quite different from anything that might have been anticipated or intended.[8]

In the chapters that follow, I begin with the roots of Imperium. What are the origins of this American "empire?" Is it a new type of Imperium (American exceptionalism again) or not? Contrary to much of the extant literature, I argue that this Imperium is constituted not around territory or military presence—although that is important, as Chalmers Johnson makes clear. Rather, until 9/11 Imperium was based largely on a form of liberal self-discipline, rather than force. This was paradoxically both a strength and a weakness. Specifically, it was the absence of a global political framework through which to articulate and enforce rules and rule that made the "empire" of Hardt and Negri a rather fragile construct, one of sovereign, consuming individuals rather than autonomous, national states that might be relied on to control miscreants and troublemakers. Herein are to be found the contradictions that made 9/11 possible. Self-regulation in human affairs is more of a myth than a miracle.

In chapter 3 I address globalization and its role in Imperium. Most discussions of globalization focus on the technological and economic concomitants of capitalism's expansion over the past few decades and often bemoan the loss of political and cultural distinctiveness that arises as a result. Although both technology and finance are instrumental to globalization, I argue that the *social* consequences, especially in terms of relations disrupted by "creative destruction," are much more critical in explaining contemporary disorder, violence, and events such as 9/11. Resistance to globalization does not arise from opposition to modernity—indeed, social movements are fully modern—but rather from threats and changes to the status, privileges, and rights of groups, social forces, and classes.[9]

In chapter 4 I turn to homeland and the evocative claim articulated in the 9/11 Commission Report that "the American Homeland is the Planet." This notion gives voice to the extent to which America's foreign interests are not only global but also deeply imbricated in the country's domestic life. In 1983 the bombing of the U.S. Marine barracks in Beirut by Hezbollah was regarded largely as a foreign policy disaster, but it hardly had an effect within the United States; today, bombings in London and Madrid—indeed, even the arrests of putative bombers—are a signal for increased vigilance and paranoia across the United States. In pursuit of national security, moreover, U.S. police forces have joined hands not only with the Federal Bureau of Investigation (FBI) but also with the Central Intelligence Agency (CIA), NSA, and other intelligence agencies, and the FBI itself has established offices in some forty-odd cities around the world. Imperium never rests; it cannot afford to relax.[10]

In chapter 5 I question whether the events of 9/11 truly constituted a Schmittian "exception." Carl Schmitt's invocation of the exception was directed at situations that could not be addressed by ordinary constitutional or parliamentary means, but rather only by the executive acting in extraconstitutional form. During the Cold War, nuclear attack was widely regarded as constituting such a condition. Although the federal and other U.S. governments made detailed plans for reconstitution during the postwar period, nuclear war would have destroyed (or could destroy, in the future) much of American society, leaving both its material and political infrastructures in ruins, resulting in exceptional circumstances. Yet even if multiplied several times and involving atomic weapons, future terrorist attacks (as depicted, for example, in the television series *24*) would not qualify as "exceptions," notwithstanding their constant presentation as omnipresent threats by near-omnipotent forces.[11]

All of those laws, policies, and actions devised and implemented following 9/11 have emerged, of course, within the context of a capitalist political economy, one that has been internationalized, transnationalized, and globalized. I take up the "dollarama" associated with this somewhat haphazard process of constituting Imperium in chapter 6. Although it seems unlikely that the founders of Bretton Woods imagined the long-term consequences of their institutional innovations—the shift from national economies engaged in trade among countries to a global economy edging ever closer to a unitary entity—the latter has turned out to be essential to the Constitution of Imperium. More precisely, this shift has been predicated not only on the role of the dollar as the international reserve currency, but also on the flooding of the world with excess dollars that have been used to support and sustain the U.S. economy. For economic reasons, therefore, Imperium is built on global dollarization, and the fragility of this foundation is now becoming only too apparent, as the dollar declines, oil prices rise, and bundled mortgage securities, purchased by unsuspecting buyers all over the world, become worthless.[12]

Why has it been regarded as necessary to establish a legal basis for Imperium and the policies and actions associated with it? This is the question I attempt to answer in chapter 7, on legalization. Although international law continues to be regarded with great suspicion and cynicism by some, especially members of the Bush administration and the Right, many of the world's people take it quite seriously. And even though law is only as effective as its enforcement, the general notion that it means something—for instance, as understood by the phrase "equal treatment before the law"—is a powerful one, even if not always practiced. When countries make commitments to observe international laws and to write those commitments into domestic law, citizens take them seriously and sometimes act collectively to pressure governments to behave accordingly. Imperium cannot be based solely on force, punishment, and threats, which, as is only too evident, engender resistance and violence. Thus, the attempt to create a Constitution of Imperium serves not only to frame legal principles and practices "beyond international law" and to legitimate them, but also to establish precedents for the future.[13]

To conclude, in chapter 8 I peer into the long "twilight." As the outcome of the invasion and occupation of Iraq, accompanied by periodic threats to attack Iran, remains uncertain, the imperial pretensions of the Bush administration generate growing disquiet and opposition around the world. What is likely to happen to Imperium? Is the world headed for global fracture and all that implies, or might Imperium be sustained? I argue that we face a crisis and transition of states and markets from a somewhat "meta-stable" condition to something else, and that this is not altogether dissimilar from the changes that wracked Europe in the sixteenth and seventeenth centuries. Those changes had effects that were, at the time, hardly imaginable.

Readers should not regard this book as either a history or a legal brief; I am neither a historian nor a legal scholar. Instead, what I attempt here is the mapping of a set of arguments regarding historical and systemic change, as well as the role of agency, especially as they operate during the first part of the twenty-first century. I try to suggest how, in genealogical rather than Whiggish fashion, Imperium is a consequence of these conditions and actions, albeit not in any clearly intentional fashion. My arguments draw on various literature about international relations, politics, sociology, political economy, history, and social theory. If I do not always cite specific authors or sources, it is not because they are not important, but rather because this book is more of an effort to divine where the global polity has been and where it might be headed in the next few decades. What the world might look like then is none too clear; as Zhou Enlai is reputed to have said to Henry Kissinger when asked about the significance of the French Revolution, "It is too soon to tell."[14]

Chapter Two

Roots

What, then, *is* "Imperium?" As I use the term in this book, it connotes a heteronomous system of political, social, and economic entities—including not only states but also economic organizations, civil society groups, and social movements—subject to the instrumental and ideological rules arising from a single locus of power and authority. Imperium is not a world state, although it has some of the features of one, nor is it a classical territorial empire, although it can and has occupied certain territories as an element of its rule. And Imperium is not merely an economic system, bound together through an integrated global network of accumulation and exchange, although the global capitalist economy is a dominant structural feature. Imperium's rules and rule emanate from Washington, D.C., but its institutions and practices depend on at least a modicum of support from other centers of authority, such as Europe, Japan, China, and Russia.[1]

Imperium wields certain attributes of the sovereignty that, according to Michel Foucault, was displaced some centuries ago by governmentality, yet it is also deeply engaged in both governance and the management of populations and societies. Under the administration of George W. Bush in particular, Imperium has abjured certain constitutive elements of global neoliberalism, especially aspects of multilateral governance, while asserting greater regulatory authority—often through military force and economic threats—over its allies, satrapies, and vassals. Imperium thus adds an additional layer of rule and rules to those that already exist at the municipal (national) and international levels, and it defines in overt terms what is permitted and what is forbidden from the perspective of its own interests. In this respect, Imperium is less about the territorial control and direct rule exercised by the European empires of the nineteenth and twentieth centuries and more about imposing, where necessary, the discipline that is lacking under self-regulating markets.[2]

Imperium did not emerge *ex nihilo* on September 12, 2001. Its discursive sources are to be found in the religious origins, both Puritan and Anglican, of the United States; its more recent material prerequisites in the Bretton Woods system formulated during World War II; its ideological and structural features in the economic crisis of the 1970s; and its current organization and institutionalization in the phenomenon called "globalization." However, whereas the settlers of the British colonies in New England thought in terms of fostering God's kingdom on Earth through individual purification and infusion of the spirit, Imperium's progenitors have sought to purify welfare state capitalism through the construction of the sovereign, individual consumer, thereby diffusing and infusing capital's kingdom on Earth. In structural and teleological terms, the Puritan and neoliberal visions are not that different, and there is an interesting conjunction between the predispensational millennialism of various evangelical and fundamentalist Protestants and American visions of a global, liberal, capitalist world.[3]

The conventional story of world politics after 1945 is well known: The United States was the only industrial power left standing; it possessed the diplomatic, military, and economic might to build what came to be called the "Free World"; and it saved Europe from invasion and conquest by the "Soviet Bloc," comprising the Soviet Union and its satellites, while fostering liberty and prosperity. To this we can add the triumphalism of the Cold War's end, supposedly brought about almost single-handedly by the discursive powers of President Ronald Reagan and the imagined threat of the Strategic Defense Initiative. Yet Bretton Woods, the United Nations (UN), the North Atlantic Treaty Organization (NATO), the World Bank, the International Monetary Fund (IMF), and all of the other institutions and appurtenances of the West came from somewhere. In 1945 the opportunity to shape, mold, and manage postwar international relations appeared to be wide open, but this new international architecture was built on the social foundations of the United States, which even then were over three hundred years old. Those social foundations were themselves deeply rooted in the European wars and social struggles of the Protestant Reformation.

To put the point another way, although today's international institutions are the product of negotiation, bargaining, pressure, and coercion among post–World War II national states and governments, those institutions were structured according to American ideas, practices, and wealth, whose origins were hardly recent. This is most evident in the organization of the UN, which replicates, albeit not precisely, the bicameral legislature of the U.S. Congress, with a somewhat autonomous executive; it can be seen in other places as well. Such homologies did not emerge with Imperium in mind—the immediate goal was to cement American dominance and prevent a return to the conditions of the Great Depression—but they almost certainly contributed to its conditions of possibility.[4]

Notions of a continental American empire date back at least as far as Thomas Jefferson's musings, if not earlier, while plans for a hemispheric empire were bruited about widely during the nineteenth century. In those days imperialism was considered a noble endeavor by many Americans—so long as it did not involve attempts, by countries such as Great Britain, to restore their rule over the United States or the Western Hemisphere. Imperialism brought civilization and civil behavior to the frontiers and nonwhite races of the world and provided resources and markets for the growing economies of Europe and the United States. Americans, believing their country to be an exemplar of virtuous behavior and a template for others, nonetheless discovered that others did not necessarily wish to be enlightened or rescued. Military force thus became an essential part of the conversion process, even as the direct annexation of occupied territories such as Cuba and the Philippines was avoided. Instead, the United States constructed a *commercial* empire, whose *sine qua non* was trade, markets, and "Open Doors."[5]

Yet by the middle of the twentieth century empire seemed distasteful to most Americans, and even before the end of World War II the United States was already pressing its European allies to let go of theirs. While this demand was articulated in Wilsonian terms in the 1941 Atlantic Charter—self-determination of peoples—considerations of trade, wealth, and control were as, if not more, important in this push. Dealing with relatively weak states would render diplomacy and influence much easier, and terms of trade more advantageous, than having to haggle with imperial aggregations in control of colonial militaries and markets. Furthermore, the restructuring of "triangular trade" among colonies, Europe, and America, whereby goods and raw materials flowed through the colonial metropole for foreign exchange purposes, would greatly benefit the United States. No one could have anticipated that so many new countries would become independent during the 1950s and 1960s—in particular, most Western scholars and diplomats could not imagine independence for African colonies much before the 1970s or 1980s—but in the context of the Cold War, the breakup of the British, Dutch, and French empires had consequences far beyond anyone's reckoning.[6]

Philosophically and intuitively, Americans seemed to believe that conversion of others to the American version of democratic capitalism—based on the virtues of reason, high individualism, and self-interest—could accomplish what physical conquest and direct rule could not, what might be called "soft empire." If others could become more like America and become more American in both mental and material terms—even, and often, as low-cost labor in the international division of labor—they would accumulate wealth, acquire material goods, and find "life, liberty, and the pursuit of happiness." Class and social conflict would disappear, as was claimed to have happened in the United States, with people's energies diverted from incalculable passions to quantifiable interests. Moreover, by applying the American model of consumer choice to politics and calling it "democracy," individuals would not gravitate toward collective mobilization and challenges to the social order. The regulatory stability necessary for capitalism to flourish could be established, and a virtuous circle would be closed. We need not detail here how notions of conversion to economic "truth," later given scientific legitimacy by the academic and intellectual adherents of development theory, tended to fail more often than succeed.[7]

We might note, however, that "capitalism in one country" suffers from a number of structural shortcomings. First, as Fred Block points out, with few exceptions, markets constrained by national boundaries are too small to absorb the full output of their industrialized production, which tends to create surpluses, dumping, and recession. Hence, although foreign investors can extract wealth from small economies, the scale of national consumption cannot support the labor force required for "take-off" of the economy in the absence of export markets. Consequently, in most places the material base for Americans' idealized social and political order is constrained and cannot develop. Instability rears its head repeatedly as the middle class faces declining fortunes and comes to oppose domestic elites. Second, within such limited markets, governments create sui generis national rules and regulations—which often favor domestic elites and facilitate various forms of rent-seeking—thereby retaining substantial autonomy in shaping the country's political economy. Although sanctions, threats, and even military violence can be wielded against governments that exercise such prerogatives—see, for example, the story of Iran from 1950 to 1953—the laws passed by a country's legislature or leadership can take many forms, often disadvantageous to foreign producers and investors. Not only does such variation among countries impose high transaction costs on foreign investors and create obstacles to trade, it also facilitates gestures of nationalism and defiance against foreigners.[8]

The Bretton Woods system, and the institutions and practices to which it gave rise, were meant to address these, as well as other, political and economic obstacles to internationalization of American capitalism and its rule and rules. First, the United States sought to foster its comparative advantage through an international division of labor, tariff reductions, balance of payments assistance to countries in trouble, and other standardized trade rules. With the expectation that America would maintain a major technological lead over other countries for the indefinite future, comparative specialization in production and export of advanced goods, as well as import of raw materials, would be of particular benefit to the United States. Second, Bretton Woods and associated programs put in place ever more standardized rules of policy and practice. These were to be adopted and implemented domestically by national governments, which would facilitate transnational accumulation on the one hand, while constraining nationalistic acts of resistance on the other. Such standardization was normally rationalized in the name of protecting the "Free World" through economic prosperity, but it was always complemented by threats of punishment and perdition for those who strayed from the economic straight and narrow (e.g., Iran in 1953, Guatemala in 1954, and Chile in 1973).[9]

From the perspective of the West, the Bretton Woods system worked extremely well for its first twenty years. Organized around national economies buffered by protective political and social mechanisms wielded by individual governments, that system fostered domestic growth while providing foreign markets for surplus production. Global trade grew rapidly as tariff levels were negotiated downwards, steadily growing demand for goods and services supported high levels of employment, and the Cold War offered a means of financing the entire operation. In the

United States and the countries of Western Europe, the middle class did well and was relatively happy. In retrospect, however, it would appear that a system of notionally sovereign states embedded in a transnationalizing capitalist matrix is fundamentally unstable. Economic growth may not be a zero-sum game, but it does foster uneven development. In relative terms, some people grow wealthier at a faster rate than others, and in absolute terms, some may grow poorer before they get wealthier. Redistribution of wealth through taxes on high incomes, capital gains, and so forth, and social welfare policies can address uneven growth and differential incomes, but they also impose a drag on growth in profits and after-tax incomes.[10]

The American welfare state, thin as it was, was especially prone to these contradictions. By contrast with the 1940s, war might be good for the economy, but nuclear war would eliminate it. Hence, war could not be relied upon to buttress growth. As a result, by the end of the 1950s military policy and procurement came to stand in for any sort of directed industrial policy, and military spending was relied on to support domestic growth, exports, and reflation after business slumps. To be sure, defense spending never rose much above 5 percent of national income, but it was distributed and targeted in such a way that its Keynesian effects were significant. The steady growth in military budgets, the constant upgrading of high-technology weapons systems, and the export of defense goods required for constant mobilization offered a second-best strategy to total war.[11]

Herein lies the secret of Imperium: The post–World War II expansion of the U.S. "sphere of influence" was heavily contingent on the dollar's status as the international reserve currency and as a hedge against the (then) soft and deflationary tendencies of other monies. In the early postwar years, there were too few dollars in international circulation to grease the wheels of international trade; thus programs such as the ill-fated loan to Great Britain, the Truman Doctrine, the Marshall Plan, the Mutual Security Agency, and the various military aid programs that were later subsumed into the U.S. Agency for International

Development. But, the financing of domestic military production through foreign military assistance and the general prosperity it helped to foster turned out to be a fragile arrangement. By
the late 1960s there were too many dollars circulating in the
world, at least given the $10 billion of gold bullion available in
Fort Knox, and an increasingly virulent global inflation, loosed
by the Vietnam War, began to erode the sovereign buffering so
important to the political autonomy of individual states.[12]

The governments of Western Europe, in particular, began to
lose their ability to make *independent* economic policy when
they accepted the poisoned chalice of a dollar-based currency
system. So long as there was an international dollar gap due to
the nonconvertibility of European currencies, the flow of dollars
from the United States was welcome; once the core European
currencies returned to convertibility in the late 1950s, dollars
began to lose their attractiveness. To dump unwanted dollars was
to risk their becoming worthless; to hold them was to hope they
might be of some continuing utility, even if worth less. When
President Richard Nixon "closed the gold window" in 1971,
Europe found itself trapped. Moreover, reliance on the dollar
exposed Europe to external financial discipline that originated,
for the most part, in Washington (Britain would discover this in
1976, when it was subjected to IMF strictures in return for a
balance-of-payments loan).[13]

For many the 1970s were also a watershed in international
political and economic relations. Talk of "interdependence" was
motivated by a growing sense that the United States was becoming ever more entangled with both allies and enemies (never the
reverse). The economic crises of the time were seen not only as
something of a disaster but also as the harbinger of American
economic decline and the rise of so-called challengers, such as
Japan. Raging inflation, rising nominal but not real wages, and
high energy costs ate away at corporate profit margins and drove
the elaboration of new strategic and fiscal policies. The Nixon
administration, pursuing the *realpolitik* proclivities of Henry
Kissinger, sought a military balance with both China and the

Soviet Union through dual détente, hoping to save on defense expenditures and to expand the sphere of Western capitalism through the business opportunities that were sure to follow. Yet in retrospect, taking the dollar off gold was ultimately a stroke of genius, because it allowed the United States to in essence borrow from the rest of the world however much the world was willing to lend the United States. Attempts in 1969 to create a new, more "neutral" reserve currency—Special Drawing Rights (SDRs)—that could provide international liquidity without constant growth in the global supply of dollars, failed. Rather than weaning other countries from a dollar-based trade system, the end of fixed exchange rates actually led to even deeper integration among formerly distinct national economies.[14]

This apparent growth in "interdependence" offended old Cold Warriors, the emerging Christian Right, and the newly declared neoconservatives, all of whom viewed the American crusade against communism as central to the country's mission as well as critical to restoring the social discipline upset by the rise of the counterculture during the 1960s and 1970s. Ronald Reagan's challenge to Gerald Ford during the 1976 presidential campaign was a gauntlet thrown down to Republican internationalism which, ever since 1964 and Barry Goldwater's landslide loss to Lyndon Johnson, had been regarded by the Right as tantamount to treason. Fortunately for this rapidly growing conservative coalition, Jimmy Carter won that election. Notwithstanding his claim to be a "born-again" Christian, he provided a much larger political target for the disaffected. Ultimately, after the Soviet invasion of Afghanistan and amid warnings of a "resource war" in Africa, his administration was driven to renew corporate-military expansion and renege on promises made to Moscow (which was engaged in its own repudiation of détente). Ultimately the Carter administration collapsed, dismally, amid the revolutionary students and deserts of Iran.[15]

It was not until the Reagan administration came into office in 1981 that the firm foundations for a newly expansive Imperium were really established. Ronald Reagan's victory rested on a coalition of an economically and socially fearful middle class, evangelical Christians, and supporters of a new Cold War. Buffeted by domestic inflation and high energy prices, seemingly at the mercy of the Organization of Petroleum Exporting Countries (OPEC), and put off by the Democrats' apparent "capture" by leftist social forces, blue-collar labor began to shift its loyalties to the Republican Party. Reagan was not an especially religious man, but he gave voice to the values of those who felt that white Anglo-Protestant hegemony was under threat. Finally, militant anticommunists, represented by the second Committee on the Present Danger, banged the drum endlessly against the "hollowing-out" of the U.S. military and the expansion of Soviet influence and called for massive increases in defense spending.[16]

During the Reagan administration, the foundation for the road to global neoliberalism was also laid down. Both rhetorically and instrumentally, Reagan's "new economic policy" facilitated a shift of domestic political power away from what are now called "blue" states to "red" ones. In order to "squeeze" war- and energy-related inflation out of the American economy, the newly monetarist Federal Reserve Board, led by Paul Volcker, raised interest rates to historically unprecedented levels, triggering a vicious recession. The Steel Belt began to rust, and American factories and industries began their long trek offshore. Perhaps ironically, high interest rates also made the dollar much more attractive to foreigners, allowing the U.S. government to borrow the funds to increase defense spending even as growing budget deficits and tax cuts were being used to "strangle" social spending. A third policy, unrelated to rising interest rates but linked to wages, was the administration's determination to follow in the footsteps of British Prime Minister Margaret Thatcher and reduce the power of labor unions, most clearly seen in Reagan's breaking of the 1981 air controllers' strike. Finally, a fourth element, which also facilitated downward pressure on wages, involved turning a blind eye to the growing numbers of immigrants, both legal and illegal, seeking refuge from U.S.-supported wars in Latin America, Asia, and other parts of the world.[17]

The impacts of the Reagan recession extended far beyond the United States, Europe, and Japan, engulfing less-developed countries (LDCs) and even some communist ones, such as Yugoslavia. Many of these had, somewhat recklessly but at the instigation of international banks and financial institutions, incurred high levels of foreign debt during the fat years of the 1970s by borrowing surplus petrodollars at low interest rates. But the supply of oil money dried up as high oil prices and recession triggered a collapse in demand and a subsequent decline from $30 to $10 per barrel (in current dollars), breaking the market power of OPEC and forcing its members not only to dip into their foreign reserves but also to take on loans to pay their bills. Moreover, because LDC debts were denominated and payable in dollars, and dollars could be earned only through foreign trade, the recession imposed a double whammy. Demand for their products—mostly raw materials—collapsed, depressing foreign exchange earnings. To avoid default they had to roll over old loans at much higher interest rates, with interest payments pushing them even deeper into debt. To avoid mass default of LDC loans, which it was feared might bring down the world's economic system, the IMF and World Bank offered rescue, but only on stringent terms—"structural adjustment"—that put developing countries on notice that they would be subject to ever stricter requirements and fiscal discipline.[18]

The upshot of the Reagan recession was twofold. First, it helped to finance the "Second Cold War" through foreign borrowing, deindustrialization, and rapid growth in the high technology industry, which throughout much of the 1980s and 1990s was centered in the United States. Even though Japan was able to greatly increase the efficiency of Fordist industrialization through "just-in-time" and flexible production patterns and appeared to pose a threat to U.S. global economic dominance, it was the "information" industries that ultimately represented the next wave of capitalist development. Second, by making the

American economy an even greater engine of global economic growth than it had been before—facilitated in part by an ever-growing flood of dollars abroad paying for insatiable domestic consumption—foreign producers became more and more dependent on access to the U.S. market and its voracious but penny-wise consumers.[19]

This last point is tricky. The conventional perspective on American budget and current account deficits and foreign debt has been that they represent a serious, long-term structural weakness that will sooner or later result in a significant devaluation of the dollar, if not its outright collapse. Yet the traditional responses to such a problem—reduced spending and consumption or higher interest rates—are largely unavailable. Anything the United States might do to raise interest rates to attract inward investment and bolster its currency, should dollar dumping begin, would trigger a serious worldwide recession. That in turn would depress demand and further exacerbate the downturn. For the time being, the Federal Reserve has decided not to worry about inflation and has instead resorted to lowering interest rates and socializing big investor risk in an effort to buffer the domestic economy. A growing global credit squeeze appears, however, to pose serious obstacles to any available strategies.

There is another way to look at American debt and deficits: as a tax on the rest of the world, substituting for the revenue reductions resulting from George W. Bush's tax cuts. For the moment the major taxpayers are Japan and the People's Republic of China, although Europe and others are paying, too. They, as well as private investors, continue to buy U.S. Treasury securities and other American properties, if only because there is little else they can do with their surplus dollars. American creditors could, of course, put their money into hedge funds and the like, which some have been doing, but such speculative activity has become quite risky, as evidenced by the collapse of the mortgage securities market. Treasury bonds remain much safer and pay interest, even if the latter, too, must be rolled over into additional bond purchases. No one seriously expects that the

$10 trillion U.S. debt—of which as much as $4 trillion may be owed to foreigners—will ever be paid off, anymore than anyone believes that the more than $2 trillion LDC debt will be redeemed. But U.S. creditors are too locked into the trade-off—accepting dollars in exchange for access to U.S. markets—to defect. Indeed, the United States may actually have greater leverage with the debt than without. Remember the old saw: If you owe the bank $1,000, it's your problem; if you owe the bank $1 billion, it's the bank's problem. Thus, even though the United States is now the world's greatest debtor, almost everyone's economic well-being relies on avoiding American default or recession. Not everyone is sanguine about this state of affairs. (More on this conundrum in chapter 6.)[20]

What about the end of the Cold War? Was that not significant for the rise of Imperium? Perhaps—but it was not as central as many might think. In retrospect, the collapse of the Soviet Union in 1991 was probably due more to internal contradictions in its centrally planned economy and a loss of faith in its ruling ideology than anything attributable to Ronald Reagan. The disappearance of the Soviet Bloc did, however, pull down one of the central pillars supporting America's program for shaping the global polity. The strategic aspects of the Cold War were central to the construction of a "semiglobal" American system of governance, which could not have been accomplished otherwise. To be sure, the repeated crises during the decades of the Cold War were only too real and dangerous, given the size of the nuclear arsenals on both sides and the uncertainty about whether they might, accidentally or deliberately, be fired off. In the final analysis, however, it was not the prosecution of the Cold War that mattered, but the apparent disappearance of what seemed to be the only highly militarized social challenger to democratic capitalism. (China may yet offer such an alternative in the future.) The mortal threat posed by the USSR vanished and, with it, the rationale for the enormous and baroque military machine so expensively and laboriously built up over forty-five years.[21]

The loss of the enemy generated not only an existential crisis for the United States but also a budgetary one. By the beginning of the 1990s defense spending and its associated industries had become an integral part of the U.S. economy, rather than something that could be easily reduced. Sporadic attempts to cut the military budget through base closures, reductions in weapons systems orders, and cancellation of costly projects failed to free up funds for social or other national needs, inasmuch as the country was running significant budget deficits. What reductions in military spending did do, however, was to throw politically important parts of the country into recession, as defense corporations shut down plants and reduced their workforces. This had an especially strong impact on southern California, with significant electoral consequences for George H. W. Bush, who saw the state's fifty-four electoral votes go to Bill Clinton. That lesson was not lost on either party.[22]

But this is putting the point too simply: Soviet communism ought to be seen as the second or third in a series of twentieth-century efforts to buffer the explosive impacts of capitalism and modernity (fascism/Nazism, communism/socialism, social democracy). For the United States in particular, the importance of the Soviet Bloc lay in its real or imagined threat to Western capitalism as a system. In the name of security, Europe, Japan, Australia, New Zealand, South Korea, and others yoked their destinies and economies to that of the United States. A few countries—Sweden, Austria, Switzerland—chose to remain politically "neutral" but were nevertheless drawn into the American-led Western economic system. The coupling of security and economy was evident in U.S. doubts about Western European efforts to construct an "independent" military force, beginning with the European Defense Community in the 1950s and most recently repeated during this decade, as well as France's feeble efforts to assert its autonomy from NATO with its nuclear *force de frappe*. No one felt secure enough to break entirely with the United States; certainly no one could afford the economic risk of doing so. Security became the rationale for Western economic integration; security and economic integration both came to depend on the United States.

Perhaps most effectively, the United States was able to use military procurement as a form of military Keynesianism, through the corporate defense sector. This provided a significant element in the foundation of an economic system that became dependent on the dollar and the American industrial base. Integration among U.S. allies was accomplished, among other means, by financing much of the Western defense effort through American loans and grants, often requiring allies to sign contracts that mandated purchase of American goods and military supplies, and building a massive war machine to provide not only a "nuclear umbrella" but also conventional extended deterrence to Europe and Japan. The allies in the various U.S.-led alliances were free to choose, but they were in essence "captive nations," albeit with considerably more autonomy than their Soviet-ruled counterparts in Eastern Europe.

To repeat: What is at issue here is not whether the Soviet Union was a security threat to the West—reasonable arguments have been made on this matter, both pro and con—but rather the economic consequences of the methods used to prosecute the Cold War. We can hardly deny that by the 1980s (if not earlier) the contrast between the moribund Soviet economic system and that of the West was a stark one (Team B notwithstanding). In purely military terms, the Soviet Bloc appeared to be sufficiently matched to the West, leaving few willing to risk all-out war; in terms of economic growth based on consumer demand, there was no contest. Moreover, although the cumulative effect of the tens of trillions of dollars spent during the Cold War, moving through the U.S. economy, was especially significant in parts of the country seen as electorally critical by both Republicans and Democrats, the multiplier effect of such expenditures was national, with important ramifications for many sectors and places. By contrast, the Soviet Union had its closed defense-based cities, which provided employment and handsome incomes for many millions of people, but the relative lack of consumer goods meant that such money went into savings accounts and barely flowed through the civilian sector.[23]

But a defense-based foundation does not a house make. It required a decade of economic crisis (the 1970s) and another decade of economic restructuring (1980s) to fully prepare for the construction of globalization and Imperium. By 1990 the structural framework for an integrated global economy was almost completely in place, and it only took the collapse of the single remaining alternative to capitalism to launch the new discourse. "Globalization" was, and remains, an essentially contested concept. Some observers argue that the integration of national economies into a global one is vastly overstated; others argue that globalization is finished and "over." But these views give primacy of place to material exchange among states, and their advocates cite trade and capital flow statistics across national borders to argue their case. Although such observations might well be correct—statistics being what they are, interpretation is of no small account—it remains the case that the volume of flows of goods, bads, capital, labor, and information—especially *within* corporations—has grown tremendously, and in 2008 the social basis of global integration was substantially different from what it was in 1908. More to the point, it is the "leading sectors" of an economy—electricity, electronics, biology—that matter in terms of transforming relations of production and social relations, and these have most definitely changed.[24]

To put the point another way, the day after the U.S. Constitution was ratified, the country was little different in material terms from what it had been under the Articles of Confederation. Yet no one would deny that the new Constitution offered a framework of rules and rule, reflecting in part material conditions, that altered the economic, political, and social environment within which American society subsequently developed. We might also observe that the Articles proved inadequate for the relations of production and social relations existing in the new United States of America; a more binding Constitution was required to accommodate and regulate society. Globalization has generated something along the same lines: existing governance arrangements are unable to accommodate and regulate global society; a Constitution is needed for that. The Constitution of Imperium is not yet written down or widely recognized, but this does not mean that it does not exist or that it does not have its effects.[25]

CHAPTER THREE

GLOBALIZATION

Standard arguments about globalization tend to focus on flows—of goods, of capital, of labor, of communications, of travel—and their magnitudes as measures of the rate and degree of economic and social change over the past several decades. Such indicators are relatively easy to quantify, are taken as significant in themselves, and most important, are routinely collected by governments and other authoritative institutions. Yet, I would argue that it is not the flows (or stocks) in themselves that are important so much as how they reflect and affect the conditions and processes that generate them. In this light, we can regard globalization as having two important features: First, it involves the expansion, extension, and deepening of capitalist social relations, "trickling down" even into those countries and places that might be regarded as only marginally integrated into the global capitalist economy. Second, there are "knock-off effects," for better or worse, for existing social relations; these affect status, hierarchy, expectations, and politics. Which comes first—deepening or destabilization—is less important than their mutually constituting character: capitalism generates what Joseph Schumpeter called "creative destruction" and "churn." These processes, in turn, destabilize customary patterns of production and reproduction, challenge and upset naturalized social hierarchies, and trigger political and social change and upheaval.[1]

None of this is new or surprising. Under conditions of capitalist growth and expansion, as Karl Marx and Friedrich Engels pointed out, the fixity of rules and social relations cannot be taken for granted or as given: "All that is solid melts into air." What are regarded as "correct" or "civil" social relations come under relentless attack by the acidic powers of capitalism, as technological change, commodification, accumulation, and cultural change expose the fluidity and hollowness of hierarchies and networks, downsize or eliminate various niches in the societal division of labor, and open or expand others. Although there is a class character to the impacts and consequences of creative destruction and churn, the political and social alliances that develop in response to such change tend to be based on "cultural" elements—religion, race, ethnicity—rather than strictly economic or class factors (which may be why the international proletariat has never really "lost its chains"). This also accounts for the paradox noted by Thomas Frank in *What's the Matter with Kansas?*, a book that asks why those whose economic interests that were so severely affected by Bush administration policies were nonetheless overwhelmingly committed to the Republican Party.[2]

The important point is that class analysis tells only part of the story. To be sure, the middle and working classes are very vulnerable to churn and creative destruction, especially if their jobs and occupational niches disappear; depending on individual circumstances, however, some are much more vulnerable than others. In today's regime of individualized consumer capitalism, class consciousness and solidarity are difficult to foster. By contrast, the array of social forces active in a capitalist society—often described as "civil society"—is vast, and appeals to ideals as forms of interests. The result is "cultural conflict" rather than "class conflict." Thus, today's "revolt" against globalization, most visible in what is often called the "anti-globalization movement," includes a broad range of rather disparate social forces.

Some capitalists and *some* terrorists are lined up on the same side, although they deploy very different rhetorics, tactics, and strategies. George Soros would not recognize Osama bin Laden as an ally, and *mano a mano*, they are not. Nonetheless, both are part of a broad, diffuse, and growing movement opposed to or critical of underregulated globalization, with its tendencies of expropriating common property and commodifying human rights.[3]

This is not the place to expound in detail on the principles and practices of neoliberal globalization—or, for that matter, to get bogged down in debates about definitions of globalization and whether it is new or old. What is different is that today's version of globalization marks a phase change in social relations—local, national, and global—and regulation of those relations, a change whose features only became clear during the 1990s. The Clinton administration's approach to the global market order was not laissez faire—indeed, it was interventionist to an extreme degree—but it did rely heavily on the discourse of deregulation initiated by Ronald Reagan. Content to give priority to neoliberal integration and the construction of the economic constitutionalism of the global market order, Clinton's administration downplayed military matters as much as possible, touting "enlargement"—the expansion of democracy and capitalism—as the formula for a peaceful and secure world. This is one reason why strategic policy appeared so adrift and ad hoc during the 1990s. With a military configured for war in Europe and highly resistant to reform or restructuring, it was easier to let national strategy drift.[4]

Deregulation involved shifting of regulatory authority from the national to the international level, with greater reliance on self-regulation, "consumer choice" and corporate good behavior, culminating in the UN's "Global Compact." Inasmuch as regulatory enforcement was constrained internationally by the absence of strong institutional oversight, the market order relied, to a considerable degree, on the good faith and moral probity of both producers and consumers, a reliance whose emptiness was, during that decade, yet to be revealed. Moreover, the utopian vision of a self-regulating, self-disciplining world remains a strong one—apparent, for example, in notions such as "corpo-rate social responsibility"—although it is a weak reed on which to base the legitimacy of the capitalist system.[5]

Still, on these various counts, globalization is hardly new and Imperium hardly the expected consequence. Nevertheless, the inflection point in human affairs wrought by the "globaliza-tion" of the 1980s and 1990s was barely anticipated by either scholars of international relations or international law. Following the end of the Cold War, an expectation arose in some quarters that the international state system was moving slowly, if labori-ously, toward some sort of global republic, even if dominated by the United States. Talk of "globalization" involved debates about the state of state sovereignty—whether it was weakening, strengthening, or changing—and the implications of changing sovereignty for something called "global governance." Within this debate, there was also considerable discussion of the notion of "self-regulation," a point first critiqued by Karl Polanyi in *The Great Transformation*. I will not repeat Polanyi's arguments here, except to note his observation that "free markets were planned; planning was not." Updating his dictum, perhaps, glob-alization was planned; the need for global discipline was not.[6]

What Polanyi meant, in the context of the nineteenth and twentieth centuries, was that the smooth functioning of "free" markets requires attentive and extensive regulation: no rules, no markets. In the neoliberal market order that emerged during the 1990s, regulation is most authoritative at the level of political economy rather than economic exchange. Yet, such regulation is not immediately visible in everyday transactions—no one is checking what cereal you purchase or is visibly imposing intel-lectual property rights when you buy a CD. The market appears to operate without monitoring, surveillance, or intervention. Within this framework, moreover, actors are presumed to behave according to their own self-interests which, harking back to Adam Smith's Invisible Hand, aggregate to a greater social good.[7]

In other words, the proper functioning of such a neoliberal order demands self-disciplined and "civil" behavior. Capitalists must not collude or corrupt; producers must not take shortcuts or use inferior materials; consumers must not illegally download music and movies. "Self-regulating markets" are premised on a broad consensus that the economy and its rules and processes are legitimate and that they generate acceptable, if not equitable, outcomes. This occurs, moreover, without full recognition by participants in the market and civil society of the web of rules and regulations that makes the market and its operation possible. To explain this point another way, it is as if the rules of baseball were defined in largely obscure and mostly unread texts while the participants were left to play their games, without umpires, in faith that no one would ever cheat or bend the rules in the effort to win. Thus, if conventional regulation involves restrictions or limits on certain types of practices, especially those that are seen to affect or injure others who do not benefit from those practices, "self-regulation" implies an actor's imposition of limits on her/his/its own activities so as to minimize or avoid inflicting injuries or externalities on others. This is a weak foundation on which to base a global market order, much less a civil society, especially when greed and appetite are also basic to the growth and success of that order.[8]

In idealized terms, self-discipline serves two purposes. First, it ensures that actors will not egregiously violate rules, gain unfair advantage, and dispose others to do the same; this should eliminate the problems of collusion and corruption that so concerned Adam Smith. Second, self-discipline instills in actors a form of mutual faith: They believe in the fairness of the market order so long as everyone is bound, through self-discipline, to the same rules and practices. As George W. Bush told Wall Street on July 9, 2002, "there is no capitalism without conscience; there is no wealth without character." Still, if everyone else cheats, you'd be a fool not to do the same, even if it does erode faith in the system and lead to its gradual collapse.[9]

Self-discipline is also fostered by what we can think of as social peer pressure. That is, we behave in a civil fashion not only because our superegos command us to but also because those around us expect that we will do so. This form of self-discipline rests on the presence of some sort of peer group—for instance, fellow citizens—motivated by similar norms, values, and interests. Individualized competition in the market, however, pits even peer group members against one another and, in a form of individualized Social Darwinism, bending the rules, if not breaking them outright, may come to be seen as necessary to economic survival (shades of *Leviathan!*). Those members of a market order who are rich and powerful, and in positions of corporate, political, or financial authority, are often less subject to such peer pressure and perhaps more tempted by opportunities that will ensure their survival and success.[10]

As the American corporate and congressional scandals and the bursting of the mortgage bubble of the early twenty-first century have demonstrated, somewhat ironically, even those who have reaped huge benefits from highly regulated "free markets" seem never to have enough and they will use their positions of wealth and power to accumulate more. Undoubtedly, both Tom DeLay and Kenneth Lay believed they were acting in the "best interests" of society by generating and spreading around more wealth, even if society did not fully appreciate their selfless behaviors. The possibly cynical nature of such beliefs and practices was revealed in the tape recordings of Enron's traders, who, while shooting the breeze, were not at all shy about engaging in legalized theft. More to the point, nothing except self-discipline, peer pressure, cowed agencies, and an evidently minimal fear of the law prevented (and prevents) these individuals, and others, from committing their brazen appropriations and getting away with them.[11]

Thus, the ideological and material foundations of contemporary globalization create certain contradictions that also tend in the direction of social and political instability. On the one hand, it is good to consume, but it is not good to consume too much; it is good to be self-interested, but not good to be self-absorbed; it is good to be free, but not to be a libertine. On the other hand, as the market colonizes new frontiers and commodification is extended more deeply into all aspects of daily life, including the body itself, the values and institutions that stabilize society come to be seen as obstacles to growth as well as to the liberty to consume. The very notion of consumer "choice" and "freedom," and encouragement of high levels of consumption and individual self-absorption through advertising, celebrity, and cheap credit, generates a kind of libertinism that eats away at the social and institutional bases of a market society. This is one reason why free marketeers and cultural conservatives often find themselves at odds with each other. Both favor discipline but disagree about human nature and whether it can be controlled through self-interest or requires the heavy hand of a transcendent authority, such as God.[12]

Even Adam Smith recognized this problem. In *Theory of Moral Sentiments,* written and published some twenty years before *The Wealth of Nations*, he wrote that, "The idea that, however we may escape the observation of man, or be placed above the reach of human punishment, yet we are always acting under the eye, and exposed to the punishment of God, the great avenger of injustice, is a motive capable of restraining the most headstrong passions, with those at least who, by constant reflection, have rendered it familiar to them." And, he continued,

> wherever the natural principles of religion are not corrupted by the factious and party zeal of some worthless cabal; wherever the first duty which it requires, is to fulfil all the obligations of morality; wherever men are not taught to regard frivolous observances, as more immediate duties of religion, than acts of justice and beneficence; and to imagine, that by sacrifices, and ceremonies, and vain supplications, they can bargain with the Deity for fraud, and perfidy, and violence, the world undoubtedly judges right in this respect, and justly places a double confidence in the rectitude of the religious man's behaviour.

Businesspeople might meet and plot, and to expect otherwise would be naïve, if not downright foolish. But if they were religious men, their activities would be self-disciplined through fear of a higher force and future damnation. Smith, however, seems never to have reckoned with the secularization of society, or for that matter with the way in which the Invisible Hand might become not a constraint on material appetites, but rather an ideological aid to their aggrandizement.[13]

At various times, and under varying circumstances, the fragility of self-discipline in the face of self-interest has become a major issue in American politics. Consider, for example, a similar problem during an earlier episode of globalization, involving the rise of the corporation and the robber barons, the growth of the railroads and the oil industry, and the impacts of foreign agricultural production and the economic recessions of the late nineteenth century. At that time, a decline in civil behavior among economic and political elites, manifest in the practices of bankers, railroads, and corporations, gave rise to mass social movements of purification among those feeling affected and aggrieved, especially in the South and the Great Plains, regions impacted most seriously by creative destruction and churn. The populists, who emerged at this time from the agricultural heartland of the United States, rebelled against the immorality of Eastern capital, both cultural and economic, and sought the restoration of an imagined golden era of yeoman farmers, rural prosperity, and religious probity. But populism was, after a time, co-opted by progressivism, an elite, technocratic program whose advocates and practitioners imposed state regulation on the "Captains of Industry" to save them from themselves. At the same time, Manifest Destiny and the Open Door were deployed to mobilize support for America's "civilizing" mission (often Christian) in lands where capitalism had not yet fully penetrated.[14]

A similar pattern emerged during the 1970s, early in the contemporary era of globalization, in the activities of the right-wing Christian-neoconservative-militarist coalition mentioned previously. In that instance, as in earlier episodes, religious morality was yoked to the market as a "natural" institution that fostered self-discipline in the pursuit of individual self-interest, while combat with godless communism provided the rationale for growth in military spending and missions abroad. Although this coalition lost some of its steam during the presidential administrations of George H. W. Bush and Bill Clinton, it was re-energized during the later 1990s, especially by the real and imagined peccadilloes of the latter. After 2001, the George W. Bush administration sought to link military power and spending to the protection of global capitalism via a more robust approach to global discipline and in that way ensure that other states hewed to American, rather than multilateral, direction. Viewing human nature as fatally flawed and prone to violence—some might attribute this perspective to a particular reading of Thomas Hobbes, others to the influence of Leo Strauss—neoconservatives, in particular, regarded the notion of self-discipline as suspect. The combined projects of the Christian Right, the neoconservatives, and the militarists, chiefly encoded in the documents of the Project for the New American Century, fused into a syncretic formulation reflecting both ideologies and interests.[15]

The failure of a self-disciplinary system lacking adequate surveillance and enforcement became only too apparent on September 11, 2001, in a way that few had clearly foreseen. The inherent fragility of the neoliberal market extends further than ideology and consumption, for that order's legitimacy rests on its relative lack of physical risk, especially for consumers. It also requires that agents not use the channels, technologies, and ideologies that foster growth and security for nefarious or disruptive ends. As many security analysts have observed, the very tools that make contemporary global capitalism so successful—air travel, communications, free flows of capital and goods, technological innovation—can also be manipulated to damage and undermine confidence in it. A vague awareness of this vulnerability was evident, although rarely articulated, in the many studies of terrorism and "asymmetric threats" published during the 1990s. Such documents expressed considerable concern that criminals, terrorists, or other "agents" might find ways of disrupting the global market order, but it was difficult to determine where to best focus time, money, and energy—with the result that all three resources were widely diffused.[16]

Moreover, the world's security system did not lend itself to engagement with what have come to be called "non-state actors." Criminal organizations might undermine faith in the system by degrading its virtue and dirtying its money, but they would not do so in order to destroy it—that would kill the golden goose. Migrants might underbid wages in labor markets and cause social anxiety and disruption, but not with malicious intent. Diseases might spread quickly; comets might come quietly; climate change might arrive no matter what. Yet none of these offered a "there, there," and there seemed to be no clear way to address them with military force alone. This gave rise to numerous efforts to "redefine security," many of which were less than fully persuasive, especially to traditional analysts.[17]

The "discipline problem," if it can be called that, was nevertheless analyzed in terms of security achieved through force, as something that could be redressed through application of violent counterterrorist tactics—a classic example of hammers looking for nails. Thus, attacks against the American military and embassies suggested that more security, in the form of walls, barriers, and policing, were needed, yet such defenses would hardly protect against *systemic* vulnerability. Indeed, if terrorists found ways to undermine faith in and destroy the market order using the tools of the market order, they might even be able to destroy the system, although no one quite knew how this could happen. As is often the case with such analyses, agents were blamed for systemic vulnerabilities. Moreover, because elimination of structural vulnerabilities would require significant social reorganization at major economic cost—and might well choke off global capitalism if fully applied—this was not a tenable solution. Instead, the vulnerabilities of the neoliberal market order could be avoided, it was argued, by finding, tracking, containing, and destroying evil people and organizations.[18]

It is worth exploring this last point further, for the structural vulnerability discussed here is not only a central feature of global capitalism, it is foundational. Although capitalism is almost always regarded as an economic system motivated primarily by accumulation and profit, we can also understand it as structuring a social system in which individual identity and status are strongly determined by various relations among that society's members. Such relations are recognized socially and characterized by their "properties," which may be material or mental. Historically, for example, the burgher, or citizen, was both identified and self-constructed on the basis of material property, which was recognized within society as involving certain kinds of entitlements. Because accumulation and profit depend on recognized and secure property rights, political systems developed to legitimate and protect those rights.

Over time, such "property rights" were broadened to include not only individual rights in the self and what we now call human rights, but also those characteristics, beliefs, and practices that we now associate with identity. Inasmuch as identity constructs and locates the individual within society, the destruction, displacement, or expropriation of identity due to creative destruction and churn may be causes for social disorder. It is at this juncture that self-discipline is most likely to break down and generate active resistance rather than accommodation or adaptation to a new market order. Oddly, perhaps, resistance arises not from the poor and oppressed, but rather from the middle classes, who are loyal to the social system but also threatened by changes in it. The resulting social movements can be either conservative or progressive, even though their sources are essentially identical.[19]

The events of 9/11 illustrate the argument. Al Qaeda and its operatives utilized precisely the same methods and techniques to plan and execute their attacks that would be used by any corporate executive traveling to inspect a new project in a foreign country. Previous actions aimed at American targets were, on the whole, unsuccessful (e.g., the first World Trade Center bombing, Khobar Tower, African embassies, U.S.S. *Cole*) and had little impact on the market order. By contrast, the destruction of the World Trade Center shook basic faith in the global capitalist order, as evidenced in subsequent weakening of a global economy that was already heading downward in the aftermath of the dot-com bust. If ordinary people, busy with everyday activities that had little or nothing to do with the structural vulnerabilities or risks of the global market order, could be vaporized, how could faith in that system be sustained or its foundations protected? Who was safe? Who would be next? What was to be done?

Despite the 9/11 Commission's finding that ten opportunities to stop the attacks were missed, it is still something of an error to label 9/11 an "intelligence failure." Foresight and information might have prevented the attacks, but they could never, and cannot, eliminate the structural vulnerabilities of the neoliberal market order, a technologically complex system composed of innumerable networks of communication and flows and intricately organized institutions of production, trade, and consumption. The material infrastructure is fragile but resilient; breakdowns are common but repairs are swift, and there is considerable redundancy. The cognitive infrastructure, however, is less reliable, dependent as it is on a myriad of individuals who, as Hobbes pointed out, value their lives and expect Leviathan to protect them. If they do not feel safe within that order, they will withdraw to protect themselves.[20]

In fact, the agential possibilities for engaging in socially destructive acts are tightly linked to structural factors. More to the point, virtually anyone can become a "terrorist." The vast majority of people will not go this route, of course, but it is extremely difficult to determine who will move from capabilities to thought to planning to action. In the United States alone, there are probably millions capable of constructing credible explosive devices, should they so desire. Consequently, to protect the homeland, the world must be watched. The constitutionality of domestic surveillance has been the subject of dispute in legal and political circles for decades, but with the exception of communications that might be routed through the United States, there seem to be no objections to monitoring the communications and activities of anyone living abroad: Those individuals simply have no rights at all. Indeed, those who are not resident within the sovereign jurisdictions of the United States—and even some who are—are the new subjects of the Constitution of Imperium, and that constitution recognizes only conditional rights, at best. Even those must give way in the face of Imperium's security.[21]

To put the point another way, globalization has transformed the landscape of "security." Whereas, under conventional theories of international relations, states sought primarily to protect themselves and their populations against depredations by other states, globalization has made it necessary for states to seek protection against those individuals who possess both the means and the motives to attack them and their infrastructures. This change is most evident in contemporary concerns that terrorists might build or acquire weapons of mass destruction and use them on cities. Although such an attack would not destroy the state, it would, as in the case of the events of 9/11, badly fracture the market order. But, as seen in the limited successes of the GWOT, efforts to eliminate those individuals and groups deemed responsible for 9/11 and other similar acts of violence against people are neither conceptually nor practically simple or straightforward. They are much more a matter of police work than military power.[22]

The laws of war address the conduct of interstate war as well as "wars of liberation," specify the treatment of captured combatants, and limit the involvement of civilians. The assumption is that any individual caught up in a war is also a citizen of one belligerent or another, and that interstate reciprocity requires appropriate treatment of each others' citizens. What neither the laws of peace nor those of war do is to specify the "citizenship" or legal location of a new category of subject thrown up by globalization, the member-participants in transnational activist networks. The conventional assumption that a "criminal" is under the legal jurisdiction of the state in which he or she is captured renders said individual subject to the vagaries of multiple legal codes and juridical practices of different countries or the extradition process. Both are time-consuming and, as the Bush administration never tires of pointing out, make it difficult to acquire important intelligence that could prevent future attacks.

The global market has to a significant degree addressed this problem where economic exchange and transactions are concerned. Not only are there relatively well-developed regulatory and legal codes addressing relevant contractual questions, but individual participant-subjects in the market also possess instruments, such as credit cards, travelers' checks, and hard currencies, that allow them to exercise "consumer rights" all over the globe. Violation of the terms of use specified in a contract can lead to reduced privileges in or even elimination from the credit network, that is, a stripping of economic citizenship, without even the courtesy of habeas corpus. Gaining redress in the event of unfair action by a creditor is no easy task, and in any event generally takes place outside of a state's judicial system, through binding arbitration. The market is not a democracy, and the "rights" of economic citizenship are linked to individual wealth, not space or place. The same cannot be said of political (national) citizenship and the rights it might convey.[23]

There is an extensive literature on the relationship among state, economy, and security, going back to Adam Smith and Friedrich List. Very little of this literature addresses the possibility that individuals or networks operating through economic structures, processes, and practices might imperil the security of the state. The figure of the madman as head of state (or vice versa) is a popular trope, in both fiction and international relations, but this is not the same as threats from "mad" individuals. The notion that individuals could possess the capability and willingness to go beyond mere assassination of leaders to systematic efforts to threaten the state, and do so through economic instruments, has hardly made it out of fiction and comic books. As we shall see, the juridical answer is a simple one, yet rife with complications.[24]

CHAPTER FOUR

HOMELAND

In reporting on the causes and consequences of 9/11, the National Commission on Terrorist Attacks (aka the 9/11 Commission) proposed that "the American Homeland is the Planet." For theorists of international relations, especially so-called realists, this is a curious locution. For students of "homeland security," it rather fuzzes up the scope and scale of the protective mission. For lovers of science fiction, it suggests the film *Independence Day*. To be sure, the 9/11 Commission, as well as the Bush administration and others, meant to point out that protection of the "homeland"—another curious locution, evocative of certain unnamed mid-twentieth-century Central European regimes—requires both knowledge of and the ability to seek out and destroy threats anywhere in the world, notwithstanding any constraints that might arise from the U.S. Constitution. This includes states, governments, and peoples, many of whom may be "unknown unknowns." Yet there are elements of both truth and recognition in the commission's dictum: American interests are everywhere, borders cannot keep the United States safe, and threats may emerge from any quarter of the globe. Given the supposed sovereign juridical status of the world's two hundred-odd states from which such threats might emerge, how can the United States create or exercise a right of intervention in them?[1]

The apparent problem of dealing with dangerous actors, whether imagined or real, might be addressed in either of two ways. The first is by proclamation of a right of "hot pursuit," a concept that has a long tradition within domestic legal systems but no standing under international law. It might, nonetheless, be legally justified on the basis of the UN Charter's provisions regarding the right of national self-defense. The second way is based on an assertion of legal jurisdiction beyond national borders, a notion belied by the principle of state sovereignty but often exercised "under the table." Neither of these "solutions" is, strictly speaking, about states of war or international law, and neither stands as a permanent, internationally recognized rule or principle—indeed, most countries would be quite nervous about legalizing either "solution." Rather than adding to the corpus of international law—which would require considerable time and negotiation—the United States has pursued creation of a new legal structure, the Constitution of Imperium, under which the jurisdiction of the American Imperium comes, quite literally, to encompass the entire globe and, perhaps, the space that surrounds it.[2]

But whereas states are the subjects of international public law, and individuals, groups, and organizations are the subjects of international civil law, this new legal structure applies specifically to direct relations between Imperium and the world's people. There are no intermediary institutions. Under the provisions of this constitution, the American Imperium reserves the right to monitor, capture, imprison, try, convict, and punish any individual who commits, or intends to commit, an act of violence or disruption against the United States or its interests. Of course, inasmuch as no treaties or agreements among sovereign states have extended such authority or power to the United States—the effective agent of American Imperium—the juridical basis for such law is not at all obvious. How, then, did this state of affairs come to pass?[3]

As I argued in previous chapters, Imperium was immanent in those post–World War II international institutions that gave rise to contemporary globalization, and it has been articulated in the rules and regulations associated with contemporary "global governance." The manifestation of its constitutional juridical concomitant was not, however, an inevitable corollary of that process of globalization. So, although the structural precondi- tions for Imperium have been in place for some decades—some, such as William Appleman Williams, would argue for much longer—a social and cognitive crisis was required to instantiate these immanent structures. Such an event would appear as an "exception" (see chapter 5) requiring unprecedented action even as it offered "opportunities" through which sovereign power might be asserted. This space of opportunity and action was cleared by the attacks on New York and Washington.[4]

The foundation and construction of Imperium's constitu- tion then became possible through declaration and prosecution of a "global war on terror" (GWOT), presented not so much as a unilateral initiative designed to protect U.S. national interests and security, but rather as one intended to make the *planetary homeland* safe from those who might commit violent attacks against American citizens, properties, and interests. Thus, Presi- dent Bush's declaration on September 20, 2001, that "either you are with us, or you are with the terrorists" went well beyond a demand for allies in this new war. In a Schmittian turn, in this speech and later ones he distinguished the spaces of friend from those of enemy (e.g., the "axis of evil") and asserted a right to invade the latter preemptively in order to transform them. This discursive slippage did not go unnoticed, particularly following the U.S. invasion of Iraq in 2003, which has done so much to create enemies and raised all kinds of commentary on American intentions, motivations, and targets.[5]

Even though the "terrorists" of concern—Al Qaeda, its associated factions, and its unassociated offshoots—are widely recognized as groups and networks of actors that operate at a considerable remove from states, the GWOT could not (and cannot) be waged outside of a state-centric framework. This does not mean that the United States is unable to wage war on the same terrain and under the same conditions as terrorist groups—U.S. Special Forces are trained and equipped to do exactly that. Rather, the GWOT is a *public* production, support for which is dependent on public relations and capturing "hearts and minds." We can draw a parallel here with the Cold War, during which much conflict took place sub rosa and, indeed, could not be announced to the public for fear of revealing methods and exposing agents. (John Le Carré's *Spy Who Came in from the Cold* remains one of the best descriptions of this shadow war.) As Vice President Cheney and others have been wont to point out, secrets are not meant to be revealed officially, however much they might say about tactics and successes.[6]

Thus, for example, we can regard the highly publicized pursuit, death, and exhibition of the body of the leader of Al Qaeda in Iraq, Abu Musab Al-Zarqawi, as a public relations coup par excellence, on the one hand, without a great deal of strategic or tactical value, on the other. His elimination might generate a rise in public support for the GWOT—wherever it is waged—but at the time it hardly made a dent in the level of violence in Iraq (again, agency is mistaken for structure—or, rather, for the structural nature of networks of agents and supporters). Similarly, we might guess that the capture and execution of Osama bin Laden would be trumpeted as a great victory; it would hardly matter to the metastasis and activities of *salafist jihadi* groups and networks around the world.[7]

The contradiction, then, is that while terrorist groups exist and act as discrete units within territorial jurisdictions, as nonnational networks they are not, according to the judgment of the U.S. Department of Justice lawyers, subject to the legal jurisdiction of those territories. That is, members might be captured and tried within those jurisdictions, but the transnational nature of network structures places the terrorist "episteme" beyond legal reach of any specific jurisdiction. To date, a global juridical infrastructure is wanting. The International Court of Justice is empowered to hear only cases brought by countries, and the International Criminal Court is authorized only to hear cases involving individuals charged with war crimes and remanded to its jurisdiction by sovereign member states. This problem might be avoided to some degree were terrorists categorized as criminals—as in Spain, Germany, and the United Kingdom—but by labeling them nonstate "unlawful enemy combatants" and acquiring general international acquiescence to this juridical sleight of hand, the United States has created something of a conundrum: Who *does* have legal jurisdiction over such "unlawful and stateless" individuals? This problem goes at least part of the way toward explaining why the Bush administration sought to link Al Qaeda to specific states and governments such as Iraq, Syria, and even Iran; such a connection could provide legal cover for efforts to destroy the groups and their networks.[8]

This difficulty stands out in particular in the Northwest Provinces of Pakistan, which border on Afghanistan and have become something of a refuge for members of both the Taliban and Al Qaeda. Although Pakistan has technical sovereignty in this region, the area is often described as "lawless," implying that Pakistani law does not apply and is not implemented. Moreover, local authorities appear to provide protection for both Taliban and Al Qaeda against actions by the Pakistani and American militaries. What then can be done with individuals captured or arrested in this area on suspicion or evidence of being terrorists? They could be remanded to the custody of Pakistan, but there is no guarantee that they would be tried or even detained. Alternatively, they could be spirited away—secretly and extraordinarily rendered—in the CIA's low-profile aircraft to its black sites or Camp X-Ray at the Guantanamo Naval Base, there to be interrogated, stressed, tortured and, perhaps, tried. In these covert prisons, such captives have only those rights granted by their captors, whose only concern seems to be that they—the captors—will not be exposed to charges of war crimes at some point in the future.[9]

Given that *jihadi* activists and sympathizers are appearing in growing numbers around the world, not to mention the gross failure of the state-centric approach to the GWOT evident in Iraq, Afghanistan, and possibly Pakistan, this legal lacuna remains unfilled. Many governments are incapable of or unwilling to commit police and military resources to the search for terrorists, even within their own territories, and any number are concerned about the domestic political consequences and international blowback of capturing, trying, and incarcerating or executing those who might be captured. Although various governments have condemned the United States for its bag jobs, secret flights, black detention centers, and renditions, some are undoubtedly relieved to be free of having to do much more than stand by as American forces intervene around the world. Yet there is broad concern about the legality of such operations, expressed by European courts and others, and continuing struggles over prisoners' status not only in Guantanamo but also within the United States. "The homeland is the planet" thus becomes a circumlocution within which the Constitution of Imperium can be devised, asserted, and, ultimately, inscribed on its billions of subjects. And if there is such a law, must there not also be a source of such law?

The assertions and acts that accompany the creation of this new juridical entity are not unilateral as the term is commonly understood. Nor are they multilateral. Rather, they are executed with some notion of a global "common good." Unilateralism is hardly a new phenomenon in American foreign policy; it has been there, and has been applied, since at least the end of World War II, when the United States still held a monopoly on atomic weapons. Although the United Nations was organized to give primacy to the five permanent members of the Security Council, there was little doubt in Washington that at least three of the other four would fall into line behind the United States. The Cold War necessitated a greater degree of American multilateralism than might otherwise have been the case had the Soviet Bloc been less antagonistic to the West, but there are numerous examples of largely unilateral American action during those forty-five years: intervention in Korea; the U.S. refusal to recognize the 1954 Geneva Accords dealing with the status of Vietnam; and invasions of or coups in various supposedly left-leaning countries, such as Iran, Guatemala, Cuba, and Chile. Multilateralism, as a form of collaborative equivalence among states, was always more of an expedient than a principle.[10]

Such "common good" unilateralism has been evident especially in the burgeoning number of international treaties and conventions, particularly in the area of trade and arms control, as well as human rights and environment, in whose writing the United States played a central role. Most of these have been regarded as imposing no significant constraints on the United States—with the exception, perhaps, of trade agreements—although a fair number have been thought by conservatives to be too restrictive of or even inimical to American interests. Rather, it has been claimed that they are for the benefit of all. Over the past decade, however, a number of such treaties, conventions, and agreements have been rejected outright by the Bush administration, accompanied by assertions of unilateral rights and privileges. As discussed later, the sovereign may make the laws, but it is not bound by them.[11]

Unilateralism is sometimes confused with isolationism. Isolationists believed that the United States should remain aloof from political affairs outside of the Western Hemisphere, although even the most ardent among them thought that the fate of the world economy was of signal interest to the United States. But the isolationists were defeated decisively during the 1950s by the so-called internationalists, who were more interested in shaping the world than reacting to or defending against it. Still, the internationalism of both political parties and presidents might better be categorized as—paraphrasing Charles Wilson, chairman of General Motors and President Eisenhower's secretary of defense (albeit not at the same time)—"What is good for America is good for the world." America's allies in Europe and Asia were regarded as reliable only so long as they remained significantly dependent on the United States for military materiel and markets. At the same time, efforts to assert "neutralism" in the Cold War were treated by Washington as tantamount to being "soft on communism" and opening up to Soviet infiltration and takeover.[12]

Looking closely at U.S. foreign policy during the Cold War, we find that it was oriented toward states as the relevant units of political and economic action. This might seem a banal observation—after all, since the Treaties of Augsburg and Westphalia, have not states comprised the structuring entities of international politics?—but it reflects the "anti-empire" (as opposed to anti-imperial) strategy adopted by the United States after World War II. This approach sought the dissolution of the British, French, and other European empires while at the same time establishing international legal and regulatory systems to which individual countries would be subject. As noted previously, this policy was less geopolitical than economic, and it sometimes ran aground in places such as Indochina: Imperial metropoles controlled trade with their colonies and, in doing so, excluded U.S. business and capital from buying from and investing in them. Such exclusions violated the principle of the "Open Door," first enunciated by the United States with respect to China in 1899, which rested on equal access to and nonpreferential treatment for all trading interests, generally in the expectation that the United States would dominate in any open trade competition with others. The doctrine was carried over into the Atlantic Charter during World War II and eventually into the General Agreement on Trade and Tariffs (GATT). Today the notion of the "Open Door" is deeply embedded in the rules and practices of the World Trade Organization (albeit with significant exceptions, as in the case of agriculture). As Michael Hudson points out, the United States has been able to shape and manipulate the rules of this political economy to its decided advantage.[13]

Why were individual states preferable to empires (a question that has been asked more recently by Niall Ferguson and others)? Whereas colonies could be protected from American trade and economic initiatives by their imperial overlords, weak, independent states would find it difficult to resist U.S. offers and entreaties, especially when promised dollar aid and loans as well as "most-favored nation" trading status. Moreover, by trading directly with ex-colonies, rather than through the imperial masters, the United

States was able to exercise greater control over dollar flows into and out of Europe. Of course there were times when these principles were trumped by strategic concerns. In the late 1940s and early 1950s, for example, Washington supported the French war in Indochina because the latter was an important source of raw materials that earned the dollars France needed to pay the costs of war as well as to buttress the French economy and political system against the electoral threat of the Communist Party. Even so, by 1952 the United States was paying most of the annual cost of the Indochina War and a fair fraction of the military expenditures of its other European and Asian allies.[14]

Eventually, caught between American economic and political pressure from above and local resistance and violence from below, the European states were driven to grant independence to their colonies—although not always without a fight, as was the case in Malaya, Algeria, and Indonesia, among others. Yet such independence proved almost immediately to be a strategic miscalculation on the part of the Great Powers, for virtually none of the newly independent states was capable of asserting an autonomous capacity to govern domestically or act internationally. Prior to 1940 the colonial territories had not been governed with eventual independence in mind, and even where colonies were subject to indirect rule, bureaucracies were manned (literally) mostly by Europeans from the ruling country. Although educational opportunities varied from one colony to the next—France and the United Kingdom were more open to education of Africans in their capital cities than were, for example, Belgium or Portugal—the capacity of the highly educated to facilitate political order has always been problematic. Thus the constitutional orders left behind by departing imperial cadres began, as often as not, to collapse soon after independence in the face of idealistic intellectuals, avaricious elites, and misguided militaries.[15]

My intent here is not to reflect on the causes of disorder in postcolonies, but rather on the external response to disorder and the effects of that response. In Washington's view, social disorder was not only conducive to communist subversion but was in fact produced by it (a view nicely articulated in William J. Lederer and Eugene Burdick's 1958 semifictional best seller *The Ugly American*). Social order could be restored by "delivering the goods," that is, making material improvements in people's lives, albeit not via socialism or communism. The desired approach—later articulated during the Clinton administration as the "Washington Consensus"—required particular forms of "free market" economic organization and activity that could only be instituted and managed from above. Moreover, because any country that moved out of the category of "free" came to be regarded as a Soviet pawn, some form of Western intervention became a *sine qua non* of national independence for new states.[16]

The tallying up of America's allies and enemies during the Cold War took a particularly narrow form, which served to suppress political development and change around the world. Every ally and neutral was closely scrutinized for signs of incipient leftist radicalism, and any country where such signs appeared became a target for U.S. intervention. In Italy and France, advice and assistance were provided to noncommunist political parties during election campaigns in the late 1940s. In Iran, nationalization of the Anglo-Iranian Oil Company was regarded as unacceptable and led to the overthrow of the elected government. In Guatemala, the presence of several "socialists" in government and taxation of United Fruit lands became the rationale for a military coup and the trigger of a devastating thirty-year civil war. In Indonesia, the massacre of 500,000 citizens, mostly of Chinese origin, was thought to be a reasonable cost to keep the country from going communist.

Sometimes these ventures were carried out in collaboration with U.S. allies (as in Iran), sometimes not (as in Guatemala), sometimes in overt form, sometimes so covert as to hardly be known at all. In all instances, the goal was the shaping of national political environments to clarify one of two positions: "with us or with the enemy." In other words, in pursuit of relations with notionally autonomous states as a political and economic strategy for shaping the global political economy in favor of American objectives, domestic social orders could not be left to domestic politics; they had to be shaped by external forces. Henry Kissinger articulated this view most clearly in 1970 after the election of Chilean President Salvador Allende: "I don't see why we need to stand by and watch a country go communist because of the irresponsibility of its own people." The consequences of this strategy are most visible today in Africa, where almost fifty years of both independence and Western political, military, and economic intervention have left the continent both unstable and impoverished.[17]

Paradoxically, despite its "anti-empire" stance, the United States began to put back together what was being torn asunder almost immediately following the end of World War II, albeit in a differently "regulated" form. Both NATO and the European Coal and Steel Community (ECSC), the precursor of the European Union, were touted as barriers against German revanchism and Soviet infiltration—keeping the former "down" and the latter "out"—but both institutions also offered governmental economies of scale and regulation unavailable to a world of sovereign states with nationally bounded economies. The creation of NATO meant not only that the diplomatic complexities of "just-in-time" alliance construction would be unnecessary in the event of the much-anticipated World War III, but also that its members were now subject to a regulated military framework that was for the most part the handiwork of the United States. Moreover, NATO was more than a traditional military alliance in which one country promised to come to the aid of another if it were attacked by a third—the basic principle of collective defense. Rather, it was a quasi-imperial organization, as illustrated by the multinational deployment of troops in West Germany and the multinational gaggle of generals and bureaucrats at Brussels Headquarters. In other parts of the world, similar alliances were launched: CENTO, SEATO, and so forth.[18]

Similarly, the ECSC was more than just a customs union; it rested on integrated economic planning among its members, encouraged and supported by the supposedly "free-market" United States which, although never a member, was nonetheless enormously important to its eventual development into the European Common Market and the European Union. These were only two of the many "multinational" arrangements organized, fostered, and overseen by the United States, all of which subsumed a certain degree of their members' sovereignty into what came to be called the "Free World." Washington was very clear that it did not approve of and would not support any such groupings that it could not control.[19]

For the United States, in other words, it was not enough to foster a world of sovereign states pursuing their individual self-interests, as posited by theorists of realism in international relations; neither anarchy nor unmanaged national self-preferences were acceptable in practice, for several reasons. First, although many newly liberated and independent countries had undergone similar experiences of colonial and wartime occupation, they were not structured or organized around similar institutions and practices. They differed culturally, historically, and institutionally, and these differences were reflected in their political orders. In many places, traces of precolonial society remained all too apparent and often became the basis for postindependence politics and conflict. Second, any country pursuing its apparent self-interest— read here "elite interests"—would almost invariably fail to recognize the potential long-term benefits to be gained from international economic and political harmonization, preferring pursuit of short-term rewards and rents.[20]

Such states would also in all likelihood pursue preferences not entirely consonant with those of the United States and its allies (e.g., Congo-Stanleyville/Kinsasha just after independence). Finally, the "national interests" of most countries were never wholly self-evident, even to those who were in a position to determine them. Because most elites had been educated in the West, they tended to think in terms of Western definitions of "self-interest." Even avowed subscribers to communism were, after all, in thrall to certain Western ideas and practices. Thus, inducing and forcing notionally sovereign states into following externally determined rules and practices had the advantage of reducing transaction costs for foreign powers and investors as well as offering rich opportunities to help shape domestic regulatory systems.[21]

Efforts to construct these new political spaces and to standardize the rules of political economy were never easy or entirely successful. Nor were autonomy and sovereignty easily transferred from individual states to larger supranational systems of management and rule. And it can hardly be said that there was a coherent plan or design for facilitating such standardization of regulation or transfers of sovereignty. The end result was neither fish nor fowl, neither sovereign state nor empire, something akin to what the theorists of functionalism thought might emerge from international collaboration on the one hand, with a converging ideology and normative base on the other.[22]

This project of reconstruction achieved its greatest success in Western Europe, out of which emerged the European Union. Today's EU is a supranational entity, deeply integrated with the United States in myriad ways, economic, political, and cultural. Increasingly the EU is subject to sets of regulations and practices that are broadly in keeping with American interests and preferences, although often balanced or countered by EU demands and initiatives. The union is also wealthy enough to support or finance many global projects and initiatives that serve common Northern objectives. American neoconservatives are quick to dismiss the EU as weak, fragmented, and a continuing burden on the United States, but they fail to consider the alternatives, which would probably be much more costly. While there is a temptation to regard the EU as a potential "superstate," and even as a future challenger to American power and domination, today it is hardly autonomous or sovereign in any kind of conventional or traditional sense. Certainly Europe and the United States do not always see eye-to-eye on issues of common concern or interest—GMOs, Iraq, bananas, climate change—but these are hardly the stuff of geopolitical antagonisms. Europe could, of course, marry its technological prowess to Russia's nuclear arsenal and thereby become the much-feared "peer competitor" of so many recent U.S. strategy documents, but that would be a gamble that few, if any, European leaders would be willing to take.[23]

Can the EU therefore be considered as part of America's "planetary homeland?" For that matter, what about Japan? China? Latin America? Africa? Some years ago, my colleague at the University of California–Santa Cruz, Bruce Larkin, devised the notion of hypothetical lines of national interests, which he called "bordoids." A bordoid, according to Larkin, is an ersatz border that encloses vital interests, such as Persian Gulf oil, for which the United States might arguably go to war. Of course there are many other interests that would not be defined quite so strongly, for example, American-owned factories in China or medical students in the Caribbean (here we should remember, however, that in the nineteenth and twentieth centuries, "gunboat diplomacy" was often trotted out in response to seemingly nonvital interests, such as loan defaults). Yet it becomes more and more difficult to decide where to draw those bordoids. After all, following 9/11, were not the deep fastnesses of Afghanistan's deserts and mountains brought within America's bordoids? By contrast with Israel, the United States is unlikely to launch hostilities in pursuit of one or two kidnapped soldiers, but it is fully capable of conducting war by other means, and it has often done so.[24]

This, then, is where juridical territory becomes entangled with regulatory jurisdiction. "Homeland security" has come to define the spaces within the juridical boundaries of the American state, yet it appears that these spaces can be sealed off only at a political and economic cost much greater than most seem willing to pay. The newly stringent border policies being implemented by U.S. authorities and imposed on the rest of the world are already generating a considerable amount of distress at home and abroad. For example, during recurrent congressional and public debates over the status and fate of undocumented migrants living within the fifty American states, a great deal was made about preventing the "penetration" of the country from the south, with the goal not only of reducing migrants' supposed economic burden on the public treasury but also of keeping out putative terrorists. Yet those few individuals arrested on suspicion of terrorist links or intentions have been apprehended mostly at or near the U.S.–Canadian border; on the whole, increased surveillance at American ports and points of entry has not led to the apprehension of many confirmed terrorists. For some, this nevertheless implies that for every suspect stopped at the border, there must be several who manage to penetrate the homeland (since the number of illegal border-crossers is larger than the number of legal migrants or those apprehended). In that light, it would seem to make much greater sense to prevent such people from ever leaving wherever it is they start from, be it Cologne, Kabul, or Caracas.[25]

The effort to locate terrorists abroad and take them into custody so as to prevent them from penetrating the United States is quite clearly obstructed by both the laws and perquisites of other countries. But more to the point, and as raised previously, how can such individuals be detected before they have acted? This is notionally the job of police, who are constrained by municipal law and practice. In the United States, so-called terrorist rings have been uncovered mostly through entrapment, and members have been for the most part charged under laws of conspiracy and perjury rather than on the basis of any actions. In several instances, these cases have proved to be fairly weak, as the conspirators hardly progressed much beyond the talking stage and that only after the goading of secret informants planted by the FBI. Outside of the United States, terrorist cells have to a significant degree been traced only after commission of acts of violence; it has been much more difficult to take into custody or expel individuals who are suspected of aiding and abetting such activities (although laws are being written or changed all over the world to make arrest and expulsion easier).[26]

From the perspective of Imperium, the problem is clear enough: Municipal law is inadequate for purposes of global discipline and order and must not be permitted to interfere with the GWOT. In practical terms, ignoring or superseding local law is easy enough; politically, as reaction to the CIA's "extraordinary renditions" and black interrogation sites has demonstrated, law does count for something. As noted previously, there is no law that trumps municipal law; international law applies to states, not individuals; and standing in international cases has been extended to individuals only in limited venues, such as the European Court of Justice. Of course the International Criminal Court could exercise jurisdiction over terrorists once they have committed bona fide war crimes and have been taken into custody, but the United States has not ratified the Treaty of Rome, which established the court, and is not willing to risk judgments by those who might question the circumstances of arrest and the validity of evidence (especially if such information is classified or acquired under duress).[27]

Thus we return once again to the relationship between Imperium, its subjects, and its spaces. By casting "planet as the homeland," Imperium draws its bordoids "around the world" and claims jurisdiction over all of it. Just as the inhabitants of the United States are subject to local, state, and federal law, so are Imperium's inhabitants now subject to its law. Just as national or federal law trumps state and local law, so Imperium's law trumps that of nation-states. As I argue in chapter 7, moreover, those individuals not deemed to be legally documented inhabitants of a nation-state are nonetheless subject to the global jurisdiction of Imperium. Consequently, Imperium can promulgate laws and practices that apply to these "stateless" subjects and assert them as necessary to prosecution of the GWOT.

The executive branch of the U.S. government has not been shy about asserting either the law of Imperium or its application, notwithstanding periodic setbacks in both Congress and the courts. Recall that in *The National Security Strategy* of 2002, President Bush announced, albeit in somewhat different language, that "the United States will use this moment of opportunity to extend the benefits of freedom across the globe. We will actively work to bring the hope of democracy, development, free markets, and free trade to every corner of the world. . . .

The United States welcomes our responsibility to lead in this great mission."

Although apparently benign—who, after all, can argue with the virtues and benefits of "freedom"?—this statement should nonetheless be regarded as a *pronunciamento* of intent to "extend" both law and politics of a particular form "across the globe." September 11, 2001, opened a window of opportunity through which the U.S. government was able to jump, as the political terrain became fluid and major changes in policy became feasible. Suddenly vague warnings about asymmetric threats and terrorists and rogues materialized in a completely unanticipated way. What had seemed difficult to implement on September 10, 2001, became much easier on September 12.[28]

Chapter Five
Exception?

On September 11, 2001, we were told, "everything changed." Notwithstanding warnings from academics, strategic analysts, and policy makers, what the public had taken to be a modestly threatening world now appeared to be a mortal danger to them. What had been treated as a foreign nuisance for the U.S. military and other American interests abroad was now clearly of highest concern. And what had been a largely tepid and ineffectual American response to such provocations now became more robust, active, and offensive, with the declaration of a "global war on terror" (GWOT). For these reasons, among others, the interregnum between the end of the Cold War and the era to follow—what Philip Bobbitt has called "Indian summer"—was over. Now it would be necessary not only to protect the "homeland" against enemies, both foreign and domestic, but also for the world to stand with the United States in its mission to eliminate global evil. Who could be safe so long as the tools and practices of modern life might be turned into the means of its destruction?[1]

That there was nothing especially new or exceptional about planes bringing death or knives cutting both ways went unremarked. To be sure, the use of passenger jets as guided missiles to destroy urban skyscrapers, although not entirely unanticipated, was unprecedented in any number of ways. But the events of 9/11 also demonstrated that determined individuals, working together, could use the banal technologies of everyday life to threaten and destroy people engaged in nothing more than living their everyday lives. This alone induced a level of psychological uncertainty, angst, and paranoia possibly never before experienced by most Americans, although a rational assessment clearly indicated that most were at no greater risk of being murdered by terrorists on September 12 than they had been on September 10. In the final analysis, then, what really changed?

It was Carl Schmitt who first posited such instances as "states of exception." To restate in brief the implications of his claim that "sovereign is he who decides the exception": Under a constitutional system, there are always limits to what decisions and procedures can be specified by the constitution and codes of law. For Schmitt, writing in the context of the Weimar Republic and its almost-continual crises, these were moments when no one knew what to do, legislatures debated endlessly without action, and constitutional authority was mute. At that moment, the designated leader of the state had to *decide,* independently of any thoughtful deliberation. When events or conditions exceeded or fell outside such boundaries, who was to decide what should be done? Two insights followed from such conditions. First, according to Schmitt, it was at this time that the enemy became clear: Us and Them. Second, only the "sovereign" possessed the authority to make decisions in such circumstances, which had to be, by definition and necessity, *extra*-constitutional (compare George Bush's claim, "I'm the decider"). In other words, the exception *defines* the sovereign.[2]

For Americans, most of whom had never heard of Schmitt, 9/11 constituted such an "exception." Did not the attacks amply illustrate the threat to both the American homeland and its planetary extensions, and merit military action, intrusive policing, covert surveillance, and abusive interrogation? Did not 9/11 and subsequent atrocities by Muslim *salafist jihadi* groups make it clear that "business as usual" could not continue, and that the GWOT justified responses that might under other circumstances be deemed illegal and immoral, not to say unconstitutional? And were these assaults not more than criminal acts, deserving the sobriquet of "war" to underline the seriousness of the threat? These have been the essential claims of the Bush administration with regard to both the events of 9/11 and the powers of the executive within the American political system to respond to them, and these and other, similar questions were answered in the affirmative. The president is sovereign and, under exceptional conditions, not subject to the U.S. Constitution. Although in the intervening years some challenges to them have been raised, those who criticized the very assumptions underpinning such questions were long marginalized and dismissed.[3]

Two questions are nonetheless raised with respect to the Bush administration's claims. First, how *did* the attacks constitute an exception meriting extraconstitutional action by and on behalf of Imperium? Second, what *is* the appropriate response to an event such as the attacks on the World Trade Center and the Pentagon? In answering the first question, we must consider whether and how 9/11 fell beyond the limits of the U.S. Constitution and its municipal law. As I argue below, if the attacks were criminal actions, the legal basis for pursuit, capture, interrogation, and punishment was certainly on the books. If they represented an act of war, as argued by the Bush administration, then international law should have applied. The exception arose, as the Justice Department developed the argument, because the attackers were nonstate "unlawful enemy combatants," lacking any identifiable territorial base but nonetheless engaged in "war" against a legitimate state. This, it was claimed, was a new development, both internationally and historically. The last point is almost certainly incorrect, and there is also a considerable body of international law that addresses the problem of terrorism itself.[4]

Perhaps the exception arose in the American response to the attacks—although devising an exceptional response to an unexceptional condition seems somewhat contradictory. Attributing the attacks of 9/11 to Al Qaeda, then based in Taliban-ruled Afghanistan, the Bush administration decided quickly to invade and overthrow that government, hoping to capture or kill Osama bin Laden and as many *salafist jihadis* as possible. The operation was, at least initially, a success in terms of its first objective but perhaps not quite such a victory in terms of the second, since bin Laden and many of his confederates were neither captured nor killed and continue to wander about the nether regions of Southwest Asia even today. By declaring a "global" war on terror, however, the United States gave notice to the world that America's right to pursue terrorists would now extend to the farthest and most obscure corners of the planet. But even this was old news; consider Panama, Grenada, Kosovo, Libya, and Iran. What, then, was the exception?[5]

The burden of my argument here is that there was no "exception." Nothing really changed; nothing was really new or unusual. Nonetheless, the national trauma, panic, and uncertainty surrounding the attacks made it possible for the Bush administration to declare, in effect, a "state of exception," a condition in which conventional means and ends no longer applied, in which the law and U.S. Constitution were no longer relevant, in which the judgments of citizens and their representatives no longer counted. The events of 9/11 served as both the justification for and the context within which a new framing and discourse could be constructed and inserted, one that was both Hobbesian and Machiavellian, in the worst sense of the two terms. From that would flow a set of claims, policies, and practices through which Imperium could be more formally constituted as a mechanism of global discipline and order. In other words, even if the event itself was not an exception, it nevertheless became the basis for assertion of Imperium's global authority and sovereignty, which itself must now be recognized as constituting the "exception."[6]

What did happen on September 11, 2001? That the nineteen hijackers' acts caused many casualties and inflicted enormous damage on the World Trade Center and the Pentagon cannot be denied. Moreover, at the time no one could predict whether or not there might be further attacks, perhaps even against the White House and Congress. Still, what were planes but flying trucks? And what were the nineteen who gained control of the planes but hijackers? And what were the buildings but targets much like the American embassies, military barracks, and navy ships that had previously been the targets of mobile bombs and suicide squads? Long before 2001, car, truck, and boat bombs had become almost ubiquitous in some parts of the world and, if not accepted fatalistically, they were nonetheless widely recognized as the most likely and effective approach to terrorism. Hijacking of aircraft dated back to the 1960s; as illustrated by the destruction of the Murrah Building in Oklahoma City in 1995, symbols of political and economic power were attractive targets for those with particular axes to grind. I do not mean to diminish, minimize, or downplay the magnitude of the attacks of 9/11, the death and destruction caused by them, or the larger schemes and threats behind them. What I mean to ask is, what, exactly, was the exception?[7]

Certainly what happened that day did not begin to approach the conditions of a nuclear war or even a lesser one. I would argue that the detonation of one rogue nuclear device in an American city—policy- and filmmakers' worst nightmare, if one were to judge by official reports and the media—would not and *could not* inflict the level of destruction even associated with a partial nuclear attack by the Soviet Union during the Cold War. A single nuclear explosion in a single U.S. city would be a political disaster, especially for those in power, but even several such events— or planes crashing into buildings in a dozen other American cities—could not destroy the entire society or its physical and legal infrastructures. Were such calculations the reason behind the Bush administration's apparent indifference to the possibility of terrorist actions prior to 9/11 or Condoleezza Rice's laconic reaction to CIA reports about bin Laden's activities? By Schmitt's definition, 9/11 was *not* an exception. Unusual, perhaps; scary, certainly. Exceptional? No. Assertions by the U.S. executive of extra-constitutional authority were based not on political necessity, but rather on political prerogatives and calculations.[8]

But the Bush administration went further, quickly deciding that Al Qaeda and its allies presented a global threat, rather than one aimed specifically at America, its interests, or its Constitution, and declaring a *global* war on terror. With this move, alternative responses were foreclosed, if only because any subsequent reassessment, it was feared, might undermine America's "credibility" with both friends and foes. (The invasion of Iraq in 2003 could in this light be regarded as a further assertion of U.S. credibility, which might have been questioned in the face of little or no further action after Afghanistan.) That constituting 9/11 as a criminal act might do more to prevent future attacks was dismissed as an ineffective strategy. Treating the attacks as international crimes would only expose the perpetrators to the slow and sometimes endless wheels of global justice, and they might even escape from custody. Depending on international institutions, such as the United Nations, would almost certainly not satisfy American calls for blood and vengeance, nor would it fulfill the deterrent requirements envisioned by the United States (and the electoral consequences were all too uncertain, as demonstrated by George H. W. Bush's rapid fall from public favor after his 1991 triumph in the Persian Gulf). Only rapid military action—war!—under the leadership of the United States would suffice, both in terms of domestic politics and future attacks. Yet, war against whom?

The normative basis for the U.S. declaration of war was revenge and prevention of further attacks; the legal basis was the sovereign right of national self-defense asserted in the Charter of the United Nations. Chapter 7, Article 51, states: "Nothing in the present Charter shall impair the inherent right of individual or collective self-defense if an armed attack occurs against a Member of the United Nations." At the same time, however, the Charter is very explicit about the conditions under which such self-defense may be undertaken. It also requires that any proposed action be brought to the UN Security Council (UNSC) for consideration and approval. Although the UNSC did voice support for the invasion of Afghanistan (UNSC Resolution 1378) and the elimination of terrorism (UNSC Resolution 1368), it is less clear whether this approval included the GWOT (UNSC Resolution 1373). That there were limits to U.S. efforts to expand international law in connection with the GWOT became clear after President Bush was unable, during late 2002 and early 2003, to garner Security Council support for the proposed invasion of Iraq, which, it was claimed, was linked to the GWOT. Although this failure might be attributable to the conflicting "interests" of the five permanent members—many observers concluded this, especially with respect to France and Russia, both of which had economic ties to the regime of Saddam Hussein—there were also serious doubts among scholars of international law about whether the GWOT was "legal" in any meaningful international sense.[9]

Such doubts, especially the many expressed about the intention to invade Iraq, did not deter the Bush administration. Moreover, not only was the purported "state of exception" transformed into a "long, twilight struggle" without foreseeable end, it was also extended from the national homeland to the entire planet, that is, wherever rogue states and evildoers were suspected of hiding. Unwilling to acknowledge the constraints inherent in existing international law or its obligations under such law, the United States asserted, in effect, that the world exists in a notional state of global anarchy in which, as Thucydides' Athenians lamented, "The strong do what they can." It therefore fell to the United States to impose law, order, and justice on the world. In addition, because terrorists are not only "nonstate actors" but also "unlawful" combatants (i.e., not illegal but "empty of law"), they fall outside of any existing legal order or jurisdiction and may be dealt with at will (i.e., hunted down and eliminated).[10]

These rationalizations might have sufficed in the Old West or even in the new Middle East. But a vacuum filled by power rather than law could at some point in the future prove trouble-some *at home* to the U.S. government and its representatives. In the apparent thinking of the Justice Department lawyers, better to construct a legal basis on which to capture, convict, and execute putative terrorists so as to avoid any future complications, and to ground this law in a sphere that would supersede the international. This search for legal foundations points toward an interesting subtext to the application of naked force as a tool of revenge: the changing ontology of war, especially over the course of the twentieth century.

Until well after the end of World War I, the conquest and annexation of foreign territories, whether colonial or not, were broadly considered legitimate purposes of war. At some point following World War II, such objectives came to be regarded as morally and legally indefensible—although not entirely abjured—exemplified by the cases of Palestine, East Timor, and even the Western Sahara. Today, according to the UN Charter, war is regarded as legitimate only in defense of the state and its society or for internationally sanctioned humanitarian purposes. Hence there is a broad expectation—one might almost say a naturalized stipulation or requirement—that any use of force by a state or group be based on an evident need for self-defense or protection of someone.[11]

In declaring the GWOT and "legalizing" actions taken in its prosecution, not only did the Bush administration choose to ignore international norms and laws regarding war and its purposes and means, it also asserted new ones whose normative and legal basis were neither social nor historical. But a "Constitution of Imperium," under which its actions could be construed as lawful, also opened a proverbial can of worms, raising two political problems that have become only too evident since 2001 and have yet to be resolved: *Who* rules, and *whose* rules? First, what must essentially be regarded as police actions against individual criminal members of groups and networks must be transformed into a case of national self-defense, justifying war. Second, the sphere of national self-defense must supersede the territorial boundaries and jurisdiction of existing sovereign states, so that that which is to be defended is not constrained by the law applying to and within those states. In both instances, Imperium's *rule* is rooted in the *rules* of Imperium. The discursive move taken by the Bush administration—one contested in much of the world—involves assertion of a new form of jurisdiction and sovereignty over global space, under which homeland equals planet and Imperium's rules are universalized. Thus a supposed domestic state of exception becomes the pretext under which Imperium's sovereignty is established and to which national sovereignty must be subordinated.

How does this differ from American practice prior to 1991? The Cold War focus on the behavior of states involved a very different paradigm from that which now applies. As Peter Gowan has pointed out, there is a considerable conceptual and practical gulf between criminal acts committed by states and criminal acts committed by individuals. He distinguishes the two cases by reference to the "Grotian view of interstate politics" and the Kantian emphasis on the "rights of individuals." According to Grotius and conventional realism, states are the subject of international politics, and what goes on within them is of no relevance or concern to other states, unless it constitutes a threat to other states. While specific individuals may become the embodiment of the acts of state—as in equation of Iraq with Saddam Hussein—it is normally as the representative and symbol of the state that such individuals become a focus or target of other states. During the Cold War, individuals and groups were a focus of American concern only if they came to be regarded as representing or acting on behalf of a state. For example, during the 1980s journalist Claire Sterling sought to establish a link between all terrorists, of whatever color or stripe, and Soviet global strategy. Various members of the Reagan administration were firmly convinced of this connection, but just how much control the Kremlin exercised over various nonstate actors has never been fully determined.[12]

By the same token, the relationship of today's terrorists—Al Qaeda, Hezbollah, Hamas, and others—to the states in which they are based also remains rather less than fully clear. Hezbollah, for example, is a social movement that emerged in part in reaction to the exclusion of mostly lower-class Shi'a from Lebanon's politics and political economy. By the beginning of the 1980s the Shi'a constituted a plurality of Lebanon's population and, following the establishment of the Islamic Republic in Iran, Hezbollah became a recipient of and conduit for assistance to these Shi'a. It was only by dint of repeated Israeli attacks on southern Lebanon, seeking to suppress the Palestine Liberation Organization bases in the area, and the subsequent invasion of Lebanon by Israel in 1982, that Hezbollah became an important political player in Lebanon's politics as well as an avowed enemy of Israel, acting independently of the Lebanese state. More recently, however, members of Hezbollah have joined (and left) the government, holding seats in the country's cabinet. What, then, is Hezbollah? An independent social movement? A terrorist network? A "state within a state"? An Iranian cat's-paw? All of the above?[13]

The GWOT reflects a schizophrenic view of this matter: Are individuals and groups associated with terrorism to be understood in Grotian or Kantian terms? Are they integrally connected to specific states, which might then be punished for the terrorists' actions, as is claimed of the Iran-Hezbollah association? Are they autonomous actors, for whom, because of their acts, punishment of states will accomplish little or nothing? Can governments be expected to impose the policing and discipline necessary to ensure civil behavior among their peoples, or must individuals be actively sought out, disciplined, and punished for their uncivil activities? Such quandaries might explain why the GWOT has not been a roaring success: Even though many *jihadis* have been captured or killed, the result appears to have been metastasis rather than excision, especially in Iraq but also across Europe, Asia, and even Africa. Each arrest, each injury, each trial, each death of a putative terrorist seems only to increase sympathy and support, rather than reduce it.

Moreover, as suggested by the cracking of the "liquid bomb ring" by British authorities in August 2006 and the German hydrogen peroxide plot in September 2007, clear links between cells and established groups can no longer be assumed. As is often pointed out, terrorism is a tactic, not an ideology, and one result of the GWOT has been to spread awareness of methods and tactics that may work in the face of both police power and military force. I have written elsewhere about epistemic "networks of knowledge and practice" that develop among various nongovernmental organizations and across social movements, often motivated by similar belief systems and goals and working from examples of successful tactics deployed elsewhere. Success breeds repetition, and repetition establishes new norms.[14]

If ever there was a state of exception, it is now past. Lest this sound like an instance of American exceptionalism, it is not. As I argued previously, Imperium was immanent in the instantiation of America's international political and economic policies over at least the fifty-five years from 1945 to 2000. The resulting entity was largely constructed around rules, regulations, and institutions shaping and governing the global political economy, which favored the United States. It was constituted around the policing of states through the mechanisms and modalities of the Cold War, rather than through the disciplining of dissenting or misbehaving individuals. It was generally assumed that states provided the social and material structures for any such discipline as might prove necessary, and that the peer pressure of society would ensure largely civil behavior on the part of its members (hence "civil" society).

The White House's exhortations to Americans to continue consuming after 9/11 demonstrated how important discipline is to the maintenance of Imperium, in terms of threats as well as shopping. Normal, civil behavior is feasible and acceptable under conditions of fear and anxiety only if people can be certain they will not die in the course of their everyday lives while performing activities that have received public approval (historically, one did not go "shopping"—at least, not in its current meaning—during wartime). Discipline is central to policing, and disciplined behavior is important to public confidence-building. In other words, the provision of security through police also creates the peace of mind that enables disciplined, individual consumption.[15]

At the end of the day, it is not clear that the Bush administration has been interested so much in the "exception" as in finding ways of multiplying American power for purposes of constituting Imperium. This objective is evident in the documents of the Project for the New American Century (PNAC) and the two *National Security Strategy* reports (2002, 2006) as well as the administration's actions prior to 9/11 and the subsequent invasion of Iraq, all of which are generally Grotian in tone and content. Those texts and the associated actions point toward a fairly conventional view of international politics: peer competitors, military balances, revolutions in military affairs. All are structured in terms of states, especially the American state and its armed forces, directed toward building a "balance of power that favors freedom." Consequently, the attacks came not only as an epistemological surprise; they were not even on the strategic radar. And why should they have been? Notwithstanding talk of "electronic Pearl Harbors" and "bolts from the blue," or the possibility that attacks might cause large numbers of deaths, considerable property and economic damage, and a great deal of political fallout, few if any believed that terrorists, even armed with effective weapons of mass destruction, could ever damage, defeat, or destroy a large and well-armed country like the United States.[16]

I would argue that for the U.S. executive branch, 9/11 was not an exception, but an opportunity. In particular, 9/11 offered the chance to put in place a disciplinary policing system that could secure the long-term American dominance over the global political economy and, by extension, its military advantage, as envisaged by PNAC and the White House. Even during the 1990s, however, it was clear that a military buildup could not be financed internally, especially if a new Republican administration sought major tax cuts. This goal was further complicated by the dot-com crash and a developing recession in 2001, which helped to restore the budget deficits of the 1980s and early 1990s. But 9/11 also offered a means of funding American military and economic dominance, through dollar seigniorage and financing of the resulting budget deficit by the rest of the world. Is it not a bit ironic that, despite widespread disapproval of American unilateralism, the world is in effect paying the growing costs of U.S. military expenditures, the GWOT, and the war in Iraq, which are likely to be well over $1 trillion before it is over? This, if anything, is the "exception." It is difficult to see how this happened, or how it could have come about in the absence of 9/11, although it is also somewhat implausible to imagine that such economic recklessness can continue without some eventual reckoning. An explanation of this claim requires a digression to consider the structure of the global political economy and, in particular, the role of the dollar as its reserve currency.[17]

CHAPTER SIX

DOLLARAMA

The United States occupies a singular role in the international economic system. The dollar is the reserve currency and, whenever it wants, the United States can create more dollars to pay its bills. There is nothing new about this; it was the basis for the Keynesian inflation of the global economy after World War II, during the 1950s, and throughout the 1960s. It allowed Lyndon Johnson to finance the Vietnam War without raising taxes. It made easy the small increases in the price of oil that later became large ones. It became even more relevant after the Nixon administration eliminated the dollar's link to gold in the early 1970s. There is considerable concern that today's twin U.S. deficits—trade (or more accurately, current account) and budget—combined with the global "credit crunch" and the "rise" of the euro and oil prices, might foreshadow the end of the global dollar standard. The evidence suggests that, short of a catastrophic depression, no one is in a position to go off the dollar. To do so could lead to a repeat of the 1930s, and we all know what happened then. To be sure, the value of the dollar has trended downward over the past few years, but the largest purchasers of U.S. Treasury securities have shown little inclination to reduce their holdings in any significant fashion. Moreover, in a strange turn of events, the world's greatest debtor, the United States, is able to substantially dictate terms to its creditors, primarily China, Japan, and Europe. How long this state of affairs might continue, no one knows. Meanwhile, America's ballooning military budget and the war in Iraq are being financed by domestic consumption and foreign lenders.[1]

What are the sources of the two deficits and their strange mode of financing? And what have they to do with Imperium? Domestic tax cuts have played a large role, as has recent massive growth in defense spending, which increased from about $350 billion in 2000 to almost $700 billion in 2007, if one includes nuclear weapons, homeland security, and intelligence agencies. The U.S. government borrows some portion of the funds required to make up the deficit from domestic sources, but it has been loathe to raise interest rates to bring in more funds for borrowing. That would raise the value of the dollar and reduce imports, but it might also negatively affect the economy (indeed, in 2008, the Federal Reserve took the opposite tack, lowering interest rates). The trade deficit—more than $700 billion in 2007—arises because consumers, corporations, and the government are importing more than the country as a whole is exporting (this, at least, is how the math is done). Much of the trade deficit is with China ($250 billion in 2007), Japan ($92 billion), and Europe ($120 billion), and all three have been recycling their excess dollars into Treasury securities and other U.S. investments. Until the bursting of the U.S. mortgage bubble during summer 2007 and the credit crunch of 2008, this process of revolving dollars had more the appearance of a "casino capitalism" scheme than a series of legitimate financial transactions.[2]

Space constraints preclude including much detail here, but the cycle goes something like this. First, following the dot-com bust from 2000 to 2004, the U.S. Federal Reserve lowered the benchmark federal funds rate from 6.5 percent to 0.5 percent. Low interest rates drove a search for investments with higher returns and also fostered asset inflation through appreciation in real estate values (leading to the bundling of the now-reviled mortgage-based securities offering higher rates of return). Homeowners—whose incomes were for the most part rising relatively slowly by comparison with real estate prices—borrowed against the growing equity in their houses to finance consumption, especially in the form of consumer goods, many of which were imported from China, Japan, and Europe. The flood of low-cost products from China in particular helped to constrain wage increases in the United States and worldwide—thereby limiting wage-driven inflation and increasing the purchasing power of lower-income consumers. The excess dollars accumulated by these exporters were in turn used to purchase U.S. Treasury securities, which are interest-bearing promissory notes (whose interest, in turn, is often rolled over into additional securities), bundled mortgage bonds, and other investments in the United States. The funds used to purchase the Treasury notes, in particular, became available to pay U.S. government bills (all done electronically, of course—"real" cash is not involved). The resulting absence of competition between consumers and the federal government for credit and loans allowed interest rates to remain low, which further fostered rising real estate values, growing consumption, and deficit spending. Thus was the virtuous circle closed. Americans consume, the U.S. government borrows, and defense spending grows. Whether this period of grace is at an end remains to be seen, although banks and stock markets are extremely nervous (with good reason).[3]

At the same time, growth in foreign exchange reserves can contribute to inflation in countries running dollar trade surpluses, because the recipients of dollars—corporations, individuals, and so forth—must exchange them for local currency to pay their in-country expenses, which increases the domestic money supply. To control inflation, China and Japan set internal interest rates at levels that will draw in domestic savings and allow their central banks to manage the quantity of money in circulation. These funds can be loaned out within the country, of course, but mostly for the purposes of industrial expansion rather than domestic consumption. In China, growing wages in many sectors of the economy have fostered major increases in middle-class consumption, contributing to any number of economic, social, and political problems, which might have unanticipated consequences in the future. Default of debt is the historical pattern for empires, as almost everyone is aware.[4]

The upshot is that the U.S. federal budget deficit, much of which is attributable to growth in military spending other than the GWOT, is being increased to no small degree by other countries' willingness to exchange dollars for Treasury securities. To be sure, it could be argued that military spending is being covered by domestic taxes—including those on undocumented migrants—while other discretionary programs, such as Medicare and Social Security, are responsible for the deficit, but this depends on which side of the aisle one sits. As noted in chapter 2, global financing of the American deficit and debt amounts to nothing less than a tax on the rest of the world, in notional exchange for "protection" against terrorism, rogue states, and other threats. The United Kingdom, Germany, Indonesia, France, and Spain know what such protection is worth.[5]

Two questions follow. First, is this arrangement an intentional one on the part of the United States? Second, are other countries aware of and cooperating with it? The answer to both questions is almost certainly "yes." Michael Hudson, Peter Gowan, and Robert Wade all point out that the sources of this scheme are to be found in the structure of the Bretton Woods system, in particular the dollar-gold exchange element in the original postwar currency system. No one took the so-called Triffin dilemma—the imbalance between foreign dollar holdings and U.S. gold stocks—very seriously until France began to demand gold for its dollars, and then the problem could be addressed only by an increase in American gold holdings, a devaluation of the dollar, or a shift to a different currency basis for the international economy. The Nixon administration opted for the last two in combination, devaluing the dollar and putting the world on a pure dollar exchange standard. At almost the same time, the United States also engineered an increase in the price of oil (some argue that it is oil that underpins the dollar; more on that later) and challenged Europe and Japan to do something about it. Over time, neither did very much. Their currencies appreciated relative to the dollar, but neither was willing to establish a new international reserve currency, especially since both depended on access to U.S. markets and feared the consequences of such a break.[6]

The fixed exchange rate system ended in 1973; the system of floating currencies began in an era of virulent inflation, caused in part by the injection of dollars into the global economy resulting from the Vietnam War and the escalating cost of oil. From then until today, the dollar and other currencies have been worth whatever currency traders and speculators are willing to pay. And there was really no alternative source of international liquidity and currency. Japan's economy was never sufficiently large to transform the yen into an alternative reserve currency nor, until recent decades, was it spending large quantities of yen abroad. Moreover, the domestic risks of doing so were more than the country was willing to shoulder. The euro might appear to be an attractive alternative as a more stable and reliable currency haven—this is one reason why its value has risen relative to the dollar even though Europe has its own economic problems—but rapid movement into the euro would drive up its value and quickly depress the value of the dollar, imposing enormous losses, both real and paper, on those holding dollars. (The inflation likely to follow such a move would also greatly depreciate America's foreign debt.) Everyone is fully aware of this, and no one is eager to start a global panic.[7]

In other words, the United States has the rest of the world over an economic barrel. It can sustain, if not inflate, the industrialized world's economy through the cycling and recycling of dollars, and until quite recently, it was able to depress the prices of commodities as developing countries competed to sell to the North, thereby glutting markets. American creditors have little choice but to loan the money back to the United States and hope it turns up again in the virtuous circle. It is not too far off the mark to argue that this is part of a long-standing strategy to establish Imperium. Inasmuch as the Bush administration has and does include any number of people whose careers were launched in the Nixon administration and continued during the Reagan presidency, it appears safe to argue that the same kinds of tricks applied then are turning up today.[8]

Domestic tax cuts enrich the already wealthy and encourage them to make campaign contributions even as the middle classes remain largely oblivious to the legalized theft of their artificially inflated assets. (John Ralston Saul calls this "stealth inflation," David Harvey, "accumulation by dispossession.") Deficits can be pawned off as effective taxes on foreigners, who have nothing to say about U.S. domestic politics, have only limited influence over economic policy, and benefit only in limited ways. The White House can blame "unfair trade practices" and "terrorism" as the culprits for budget deficits and pressure China and Japan to liberalize, revalue their currencies, and import more American goods to reduce trade deficits. And the GWOT, waged in all of its facets, can be financed without any attention being paid to its macroeconomic or strategic consequences. This is why "the American homeland is the planet." The world is the tax base for Imperium.[9]

Such exceptionalist behavior is not limited to taxation without representation; it also extends to oil. During the early 1970s the Nixon administration recognized that an increase in oil prices would impose greater economic costs on Europe and Japan and help to reduce their growing competitiveness. It might also redress the trade deficit (first experienced in 1971). At the same time, Washington was seeking ways to reduce military spending, especially in Vietnam, and secure the flow of oil from the Persian Gulf in the aftermath of the withdrawal of British forces in 1971. The solution was the "Nixon Doctrine," which envisioned regional security and policing by local U.S. allies. In Indochina, South Vietnam was the cop, making it feasible for the United States to pull out almost all of its ground troops from that war. In the Persian Gulf the "policeman" was Iran, ruled by Shah Mohammad Reza Pahlavi (who owed his throne to the British–American engineered coup against Prime Minister Mohammed Mossadeq in 1953).[10]

The problem was that, with oil then at about $3/barrel ($16/barrel in 2008 dollars, adjusted for inflation), the shah needed additional income to finance the purchase of U.S. armaments. The United States and Iran agreed on a small engineered increase in the price of oil—about 20¢ per barrel—in contravention of the big oil companies' desire to *reduce* the posted price. In the event, as Franz Schurmann and others have documented, the shah proved to be a "price hawk" and was instrumental in the rather larger price increases that followed during the 1970s. Of course it followed that, as Iran built up its military forces, so would its neighbors, who also had large currency surpluses to recycle through Western banks and countries. In other words, the growing militarization of the Middle East and Persian Gulf served not only ostensible strategic goals but also economic ones.[11]

In this light, the jump in oil prices since 2005, from $25 to more than $100 per barrel, becomes somewhat more explicable: It is a necessary, if not sufficient, element in the global tax scheme, for at least four reasons. First, it represents an effective devaluation of the dollar on the one hand, and a sink for foreign dollar holdings on the other. This does not make U.S. goods less costly, as in a traditional devaluation, but it does impose higher costs on other countries, which makes American products relatively less expensive (and even more so if it drives down the value of the dollar). Second, while the price increase imposes higher costs on the American economy, it also does the same for China, which is actively seeking out long-term sources and contracts for oil and is purchasing foreign oil companies as a way of ensuring supply but not necessarily the lowest price— oil producers may be less willing to lock in lower petroleum prices if there is a possibility of earning more as a result of uncertainty in markets. Third, higher oil prices cycle dollars through oil-producing countries rather than back into the U.S.

debt, creating potential customers for military sales. The recent arms deal with Saudi Arabia, which could run to $20 billion over the next decade and will be matched by $30 billion in arms transfers to Israel—albeit with U.S. money—illustrates this point. At least some oil producers may be induced to purchase American weapons systems with their newly gained bounty. This is especially true given current uncertainties in the Gulf region and growing fears of Iran. Finally, as recent quarterly reports from the oil majors have shown, at least some foreign revenues are being captured by U.S.-based companies, which continue to pump and sell a fair amount of oil abroad. The actions of the Nixon administration during the 1970s demonstrate that none of this is new. As Marx wrote in *The 18th Brumaire*, first time as tragedy, second time as farce.[12]

Does this mean that (1) the GWOT is really a strategy in political economy, rather than a military one, and/or that (2) the Bush administration used the "exception" of 9/11 as a pretext for putting this strategy into play? There are two angles to these questions. First, to return to a point made in chapter 5, uncovering and breaking terrorist projects is more a matter of dogged police work than military strategy. This seems to be the lesson from the various plots in Europe uncovered by British, German, Spanish, Danish, and other national authorities. In the case of the British revelation in 2006 of a major plot by Muslim citizens to smuggle the materials for assembling and detonating bombs aboard as many as ten transatlantic flights, investigations and surveillance had been underway for almost a year prior to the public announcement of the plot. The Bush administration even pressured the British authorities to reveal details before they were ready (as a political favor from Tony Blair to George Bush?). But police work is relatively cheap compared to war. It is tedious, less inspiring of patriotism, and leaves the suspects alive. Notwithstanding the fact that U.S. "homeland security" and "intelligence" each absorb upward of $40–50 billion every year, most of that goes neither to police work nor to human intelligence but rather to "first responders," research into protection against weapons of mass destruction (WMDs), and the operating costs of the National Security Agency.[13]

Second, as noted previously, the Bush administration came into office determined to (1) maintain American domination in the global military sphere and discourage peer competitors; (2) ramp up defense spending, especially with respect to the "revolution in military affairs," to address the "hollowing out" of the military during the 1990s; and (3) define a set of threats against which such a program could be directed. During the Clinton administration the Pentagon pursued a "two-war strategy," preparing to fight two Gulf-style wars, either simultaneously or in sequence. This strategy did not require massive growth in military spending, inasmuch as it depended largely on people and materiel already in stock. The new president and his advisers, who seemed to believe that deterrence and rule required much more, found this strategy inadequate. In its calls for a new military buildup, the Project for the New American Century was fairly specific about deposing Saddam Hussein. As has been widely reported, then–defense secretary Donald Rumsfeld began to advocate an invasion of Iraq even before the dust from the 9/11 attacks had settled. The administration's initial estimates of the war's cost were relatively low—on the order of $20 billion, although at least one estimate ran to $100 billion—and it felt confident that growing quantities of oil would soon be flowing out of Iraq, providing the funds needed for domestic reconstruction—presumably to be undertaken by American companies (the early postwar exclusion of European corporations was not just a matter of spite). The United States could then turn to dealing with Syria and Iran and, in the process, manage to sell considerable quantities of weapons to newly terrified allies and clients in the region.[14]

It might be noted here that the civilian leadership in the Pentagon had differing and sometimes conflicting goals in advocating an invasion of Iraq. Defense Secretary Rumsfeld wanted to field test the "revolution in military affairs" and demonstrate that capital (technology) could substitute for labor (infantry) in the prosecution of war and pursuit of national security. Paul Wolfowitz envisioned a "new Middle East," converted to capitalism and democracy and centered around an Israeli development pole. Others, such as the Christian Right, had the millennium in mind. The point is that a short, successful war could have undermined the old-line generals and admirals fixated on Cold War weapons platforms and maintenance of funding levels and allowed the "Young RMA Turks" supporting Rumsfeld to move into positions of authority in the Pentagon. Thus 9/11 offered the opportunity to restructure the American military into something more suited for the low-intensity interventions and actions associated with global disciplining by Imperium.[15]

Rumsfeld's strategy was not a complete failure, although events in Iraq suggest that low-tech offense is much less costly than high-tech defense, and that the former is much more sustainable than the latter. Indeed, in the longer term, overreliance on advanced technology might well bankrupt the entire military enterprise. At the same time, however, the political economy strategy has been a roaring success—at least on its own terms. The fact is that, as during the Korean War, much of the increase in U.S. defense and security spending between 2000 and 2008 has not gone into the GWOT (for example, the 2008 Senate defense authorization totals almost $700 billion, of which $189 billion is allocated to Iraq and Afghanistan). Instead, most of this money is being spent on military systems designed for (nuclear) war in Europe. A considerable quantity is also flowing into major U.S. corporations at home and in Iraq. However one might do the math, and wherever one might put the blame for insufficient domestic tax revenues, the current U.S. budget deficit is roughly equal to the $300 billion increase in annual defense spending from 2000 until today. Whether that sum is coming out of the hide of Chinese workers, American homeowners' equity, or European financial speculators, someone is paying.[16]

But much of this political economy strategy has an ad hoc quality to it, based as it is on contingency. Even if terrorism is as serious a global problem as it is made out to be, the future lies not in countries overrun by terrorist organizations (as was the case in Afghanistan under the Taliban), but in small cells scattered around the world. At some point the GWOT will run out of steam, and the current rationale for military domination will lose ground to the exigencies of careful detective work. The strategy of political economy—of making the rules, rather than just manipulating applications and outcomes—requires that new structures be developed, ones that not only rationalize Imperium but also embed it in a legalistic framework that comes to be widely recognized as legitimate. The Bush administration, servant to a fractious domestic political coalition, has been rather ham-handed in constructing a Constitution of Imperium. This does necessarily mean, however, that the overall project will fail.[17]

CHAPTER SEVEN
LEGALIZATION

The legal issues raised by Imperium would not have greatly troubled the empires of the past. To be sure, imperial authorities of the nineteenth and twentieth centuries were usually careful to devise legal systems for conquered, colonial, and other territories over which they ruled. At the same time, metropolitan intellectuals provided ontological rationales for such rule and rules: the White Man's Burden, Western civilization, Manifest Destiny, and so forth. For the most part, however, there was little, if any, effort to legalize the *fact* of empire: This was simply the prerogative of powerful Western states asserting their domination of foreign territories. What distinguishes Imperium from its predecessors is the effort to create a *legal* basis for its legitimacy, a constitution that is external to both American and international law. This requires the creation of certain legal "facts" regarding both executive authority and the subjects of that authority, in effect trumping certain juridical functions of the state and limiting certain rights that accrue to those physically resident within any internationally recognized state or territory. That is, by establishing a new category of imperial subject, the United States asserts that sovereign states lose legal jurisdiction over the occupants of a certain category, even if they are physically present within a sovereign state's national territory.[1]

This is a tricky point. Since World War II, states are not allowed to simply assert legal jurisdiction over or "ownership" of people who are citizens of or resident in another sovereign territory (such as, for example, Hungarians living in Slovakia or Serbia). A state might of course kidnap specific individuals and claim a legal right to try them. Examples of this include Israel's 1960 kidnapping of Adolph Eichmann, who was living in Argentina, and the CIA's "extraordinary rendition" in 2003 of, among others, Khaled el-Masri, a German citizen detained in Macedonia and interrogated in Afghanistan. In the case of Eichmann, this was widely protested as a violation of both his rights and international law. In the aftermath of 9/11, many argued that the wheels of criminal justice grind much too slowly to protect against future attacks, many of which would be planned in those "ungoverned spaces" where states exercised little or no direct control. Prevention (and deterrence) of attacks, it was argued, would depend on timely and effective interrogation of suspects captured in lawless places in Afghanistan and Pakistan. Bringing such individuals onto the territory of the United States might, however, set in motion the wheels of domestic justice—as seen in the tortuous cases of José Padilla and Salim Ahmed Hamdan—which would delay a final resolution.[2]

The Bush administration therefore decided to incarcerate detainees in a "nonsovereign" space where U.S. domestic law would not apply, to wit, the Guantánamo Naval Base. I will not address here the claim that both naval base and prison camp are *not* sovereign American territory, an argument that rests on a tortured logic that an indefinite lease, obtained under duress and viewed as null and void by the lessor (Cuba), renders the leased place not subject to the lessee's (U.S.) legal jurisdiction, even if under the latter's military control. This is a claim that no domestic or international court would accept, especially if offered by a typical business or residential tenant. Nonetheless, by making such a claim for the base and prison, the United States has sought to create a new type of juridical space, one exempt from international law as it applies to states and national law as it applies to individuals within American territorial jurisdictions. Moreover, by declaring individuals taken prisoner by the United States and incarcerated in these nonsovereign sites to be "unlawful enemy combatants," their notional citizenship or nationality or place of capture has no legal standing within such places of internment. Taken together, these two principles render prisoners subjects of local representatives of the authority that control—but are not sovereign over—the spaces of internment. And that authority, by declaration, was none other than President George W. Bush of the United States.[3]

As this was happening in the early days of the GWOT, lawyers in the Justice Department's Office of Legal Counsel, under the direction of Vice President Cheney's legal counsel David Addington, tried to devise the legal basis for such claims of authority and control. Their efforts were motivated in part by concern that, at some time in the future, members of the Bush administration might be subject to prosecution for war crimes and other violations of national and international law. But there seems to have been more at work here. John Yoo, Jack Goldsmith, and others all subscribed to the notion that "international standards of human rights should not apply in cases before U.S. courts" and that the executive branch's policies and actions should not, contra Schmitt, deliberately violate or abrogate the U.S. Constitution. Still, international law be damned! Perhaps the need for textual inscription and legitimation arises from lawyers' socialization in school or courts or is a feature of bureaucratic systems—one is reminded of the Nazis' careful promulgation of rules, regulations, and laws to legalize everything they did—but it might also be ascribed to the extensive legal experience present in the higher echelons of the Bush administration, even though Bush himself is not a lawyer.[4]

Why is a legal framework even necessary? After all, law takes time and, as noted by those who justify torture, expediency is sometimes necessary. Should not actions taken to protect national interests and national security trump considerations of the law—as the federal government is wont to argue in court? Is not the primary national interest the survival of the state? If the sovereign can decide the extraconstitutional exception, why does he need any law at all? By all rights, whatever he does should be legitimate even if his actions violate constitutional and statutory law. Under the circumstances of a true state of exception, in which the state is under mortal threat, would there be any hesitation to cut down, on the spot, those who might execute a mortal threat? And would not the sovereign be granted the unquestioned authority to respond to actualization of such a threat? This, of course, was an issue central to debates over nuclear deterrence, first strike, and decapitation strategies during the Cold War. Although few doubted that the president could act preemptively should he choose to do so, many questioned whether, in the heat of the moment, he would. Hence, during the 1980s debates about such matters came to revolve around morality rather than legality per se.[5]

As it turns out, legal scholars hardly agree on such questions, let alone the answers, because there are no final, authoritative sources of law. There are those who argue that "international" law is oxymoronic by definition: In the absence of a sovereign source, how can there be law? For those critics, law is purely formalistic and, mirroring power relations, is not only discriminatory but an outright fraud. By contrast there are others who argue quite the opposite case: Without law there can be no society and, since there is, at a minimum, a rudimentary international society, there must be law and it must have some effect in moderating the behavior of states. Between these two poles are any number of positions that, for the most part, need not concern us here. Our focus is on the relevance of international law to Imperium.

The problem in the current instance seems to be the argument that international law is inadequate for the "present danger," that is, the threat of global terrorism, and that it restricts the autonomy of the United States. Not only is the law slow and

deliberate, there are so many loopholes and outs in apprehend-
ing, trying, convicting, and incarcerating (or executing) a defendant that justice may never be done. When countless lives could
hang in the balance if information about plots and conspiracies
is not extracted from one individual or another, the law simply
places unreasonable obstacles in the path of those who seek to
protect people and society. Hence new "operating procedures"
must be devised to address such contingencies, and even if they
skirt the borders of what is normatively acceptable—for example, interrogation techniques just short of death—these procedures must be "legalized" so that those who engaged in them will
not suffer self-recrimination or, at some future date, find themselves in court, whether national or international, on charges of
"human rights violations" or even "crimes against humanity."[6]

In asking why a Constitution of Imperium, rather than international or municipal law, is deemed necessary for such policies
and actions, we move from the clearer water of law to the rather
more murky swamps of sociology. A constitution is not, after all,
the same thing as statutory law. As described in chapter 3, we can
think of the latter as defining the rules for *playing* a game—that
is, the rules for distributing or acquiring points—and the former
as laying out the rules that *define* a game—what forms, principles,
and procedures constitute the game, that is, its political economy
of regulation. A constitution is, moreover, a social contract, specifying the roles, rules, and relationships that structure a society, and
this contract is what, under capitalism in particular, gives that
structure legitimacy. There is no necessary concordance between
a constitution and what can for our purposes be called the "common" or distributive law of society. Reconciling the two is the
job of the courts, which do not necessarily follow strict legal reasoning (or precedent) in their rulings and sometimes acknowledge that social change is relevant to interpretation of the law.[7]

Constitutions may also be amended or rewritten to take
into account new or changing social and political circumstances
(e.g., abolition of slavery, women's suffrage, lotteries). Thus it is
possible to argue that a "constitution" reflects social arrange-

ments at the time of its writing, rather than a set of universal and eternal principles to which societies must hew forever and ever. This point parallels the ongoing conflict in the United States between strict constructionists and those who regard the U.S. Constitution as requiring contextual interpretation and application. In other words, the Constitution of Imperium should be seen not as a physical document, but rather as a set of principles and practices generated out of the context and times in which it is being written even as it is also required to generate its own legitimacy. This is how the British "constitution" has been constructed even though it does not exist as a single authoritative document.[8]

Moreover, a constitution is never a politically neutral text. From a Whiggish perspective, it may come to be regarded mythically as fair, just, and equitable—or even "colorblind," as in the widely held belief regarding the U.S. Constitution. Such claims are at best a nationalist illusion, for unless they are imposed from the outside, as was Japan's after World War II, constitutions emerge only as a result of struggle among dissonant social forces (under conditions of social harmony, such a document would not be necessary), and they tend to reflect the hegemony of those social forces that gain dominance at particular times. The final text may represent a compromise, or it may be the product of power imbalances and the victory of one faction over others. But it is never neutral. In the case of the Constitution of Imperium, the number of social groups in conflict is myriad, and their interplay is complex, for the stakes are high. The outcome of the yet-to-be-resolved struggle for authority among the U.S. executive, Congress, and the courts, as well as the opposition of other countries and the actions of terrorist and other groups—rather than the scribblings of Justice Department lawyers—will determine the fate of the project of Imperium and its constitution.[9]

We might say, therefore, that a constitution is a document (or, in the case of the United Kingdom, a set of documents and precedents) that establishes a set of ontological rules and foundational operating principles against which to test political and

economic policies and practices that support or offend the interests and beliefs of one or another segment of the polity. In the
international realm, the UN Charter constitutes one of many
such constitutional documents for something we might call the
"UN Republic," a neo-Kantian system that is surrounded by a
penumbra of international laws and regulations. At the same
time, however, two related developments have complicated what
has long seemed to be a clear division of legal labor. First, human
rights law, which states are bound to deploy and respect, applies
to individuals. In a growing number of settings, moreover, individual plaintiffs can bring suit against states for violations of such
law (e.g., in the European Courts of Justice and Human Rights).
This creates legal complications, inasmuch as states, as such, cannot stand as meaningful defendants in such cases. Thus, for example, the various war crimes tribunals of the past sixty years have
never passed judgment on the guilt or innocence of states, only
on individuals representing authority in such states.[10]

Second, and perhaps of greater importance, is another point
suggested throughout this book: the emergence of the sovereign
consumer-citizen of the global political economy, whose rights
and responsibilities are no longer fully mediated by a nation-
state apparatus and who might no longer be loyal to or identify
with specific nation-states. Scholars of globalization have talked
for some time about the "cosmopolitan" citizens of a world
"cosmopolis." It is also evident that there are growing numbers
of people who are not cosmopolitan or do not hold first loyalties to their state of birth or residence, but who also are not con-
tained and constrained by states, their laws, and their norms.
These people are not necessarily "stateless" in that they lack
nationality or passport, as was the case for many during the first
half of the twentieth century; they may even have several
nationalities and passports. Rather, they eschew close identifica-
tion with specific nation-states and are instead more closely
linked to nonstate formations, such as corporations or movements. So far this group of people is merely a social category
with no international formal or legal standing or content.[11]

"Unlawful enemy combatants" are members of this group, often living in so-called lawless and ungoverned spaces. The former connotes what is generally called a "failed state"—there is no recognized government—the latter, an inability to police—there are no effective authorities. Somalia is an example of the former; the wide open spaces of the Sahel, the latter. Such spaces are evocative of international anarchy, lacking a sovereign; in a Hobbesian sense, they are more accurately understood as conceptual "states of nature," in which there is claimed to be no effective or recognized social structure or law. Nothing, however, could be further from reality on the ground. Law and sovereignty do exist in these spaces—often *Sharia* and the sovereignty of God—but these are not recognized as legitimate or acceptable by the United States. In this light, any country whose legal system is based in part or whole on *Sharia* becomes a site in which terrorists can congregate safely and conspire to "break out" into the "lawful world," and in which effective surveillance and disciplining are judged impossible. The fear of such spaces, and their growth potential, is evident in the Pentagon's nightmares of a Muslim caliphate reaching from Mauritania in the west to Mindanao, in the Philippines, in the east.[12]

The important point here is that, according to the claims of the U.S. government, the inhabitants of such spaces have no effective relationship with international law or the state system. Not only are they outside the boundaries of "civilization," they are also not subject to any internationally recognized municipal law and seem beyond the reach of police and punishment. Moreover, they possess no human rights as such, because these are granted only by recognized sovereign states. At the same time, they have no reciprocal obligations to any civil authority or sovereign and are therefore untrustworthy. This is an intolerable state of affairs for both the Bush administration and the Justice Department lawyers, and their remedy is the Constitution of Imperium.

Here is where the Justice Department lawyers truly proved their value as well as their moral depravity. They argued that, because those captured in lawless and ungoverned spaces were subject to no municipal law, they could not be considered either legal combatants or citizens of the states in whose territory they were found. Under the laws of war and the Geneva Conventions, therefore, they had no prisoner-of-war rights or protections. And, inasmuch as there was no effective domestic jurisdiction in these spaces, they could not be "citizens" or "civilians" in the common understanding of the term. Finally, any who were citizens of other states had, in effect, forfeited their legal rights by moving to these external spaces. In any case, being "stateless," they were also not subject to human rights law. While lawless and ungoverned spaces could not be considered *res nullis* under the classical definition of the term, they were spaces in which law could be instantiated by the proper authority. In this instance, that authority was (and is) Imperium. The further result of this move was, as argued previously, to make these unlawful combatants and stateless persons subjects of Imperium and its constitution.

Does the American executive branch have the authority or right to do this (or is power all that counts)? Here we return to the debate between those, such as Hans Kelsen, who have argued for the formalism of law, and those, such as Carl Schmitt, who have argued for its instrumental origins. To reiterate the distinction between the two, for the former, law can only be constituted by a legitimate authority, which in the Lockean state form must have some relationship to the "people." Hence, although the UN republic can be attacked for exhibiting a "democratic deficit," it is notionally representative of the world's people through its member states and its laws are formally appropriate. For the latter, the state is a Hobbesian one, for which there are always limits to such a process, defined by the "exception." Yet what is done by the sovereign in the event of an exception becomes law as exceptional circumstances are normalized. Paradoxically, the sovereign decides the exception in order to put in place a new set of rules and practices that will normalize the exception: "Everything has changed" becomes a normalized "long twilight struggle" without visible end.[13]

There is yet another paradox evident here: this Imperium must escape from the earthly bindings of the U.S. Constitution and is forced to do so through claims made about and before the U.S. judiciary. This is a ticklish point. On the one hand, responding to lawsuits in American courts recognizes limits to what the American executive branch may do under the Constitution; on the other hand, even victory in such cases acknowledges the jurisdiction of federal courts. Only successful suppression or refusal to hear—the courts admitting lack of standing—free the executive branch to do as it wishes, albeit not without struggle. The White House has repeatedly asked that cases involving activities that might be in violation of the Constitution and law—unapproved wiretapping, indefinite detention of U.S. citizens, and so forth—be thrown out, generally on the grounds that revelations necessary to the proceedings would threaten national security and offer secret intelligence to the nation's enemies. In effect, President Bush's claims for the unitary executive organ also contest the judiciary's right to make a judgment on what might constitute an exception.[14]

Quite understandably, there is considerable discomfort with these claims, not only among the public but also in various federal courts as well as among a fair number of members of the U.S. Congress. The latter have, however, found their ability to limit executive authority and action problematic, because the president has declared more than 750 provisions in some 125 laws as not binding on him. There is considerable precedent for such signing statements, although Bush appears to have issued them more frequently than all his predecessors combined. Many of these statements address fairly mundane points, but the argument is the same for all: The president obeys statutory *and* constitutional law at his own will and discretion. His sovereignty supersedes that of Congress, the notional representative of the people from whom, supposedly, sovereignty emerges.[15]

To be entirely fair, the American executive branch continues to hold the law in high regard, so long as it does not impose limits on that branch of government. The United States is a nation of laws, and so the world should be. But who is to issue such laws? Based on its proclamations and practices, the executive branch holds that it has the right not only to issue administrative regulations but also to write the laws of Imperium. There is no global representative assembly with which such sovereignty might be shared—recall that the UN General Assembly is composed of state representatives, and Imperium's rule trumps both the UN and its members—and there is no judiciary to rule on the "constitutionality" of law—Imperium does not recognize either the International Court of Justice or the International Criminal Court. As in the absolutist regimes of eighteenth-century Europe, under Imperium the sovereign *makes* the law, the sovereign *judges* the law, the sovereign *is* the law.

This possibility has long been immanent in the U.S. Constitution, but it was constrained historically by context and circumstance. The Founding Fathers, after all, sought to create a political system that could stand up to the absolutism of Britain and even contemplated the possibility of a royal sovereign. Ultimately, they settled on a "president" whose authority would ultimately be decided through struggles among the three branches as well as the social and class forces represented by those branches. Where populist tendencies appeared, as in the Whiskey Rebellion or the Civil War, the executive did not hesitate to act with massive force. And once the security of the United States came to be defined in more and more world-encompassing terms—in 1917, 1941, 1950, 1991—executive powers expanded to fill newly opened political and legal spaces. These were not the spaces of interstate relations, as has been so commonly assumed; they were the spaces of supra-state rules and rule. When that arrangement proved inadequate to the task, as was judged to be the case after 9/11, the executive branch's expansionist prerogatives were asserted once again.[16]

Nowadays constitutions are written willy-nilly, as conditions demand. There are cadres of constitutional scholars and lawyers prepared, at the drop of a hat, to rush off to some country—such as Iraq or South Africa—where a new document is thought to be needed. These are much like the legal forms available online and at stationery stores, with blanks to be filled in as appropriate and paragraphs to be added or excised as needed. But they are constitutions for concrete political structures whose basic forms fall into a very few categories. The constitution for a new, hybridized political structure such as Imperium is not an off-the-shelf product, and it most certainly will not be written "in Congress gathered." Indeed, as the product of long and constant struggle among various centers of power and authority, the Constitution of Imperium is unlikely ever to appear as a single text. Nevertheless, one hundred years hence it is likely to be as "real" as any similar document under glass today.[17]

What, then, does this mean in concrete terms? Within the reach of Imperium, as noted previously, there is no "national sovereignty" as commonly understood: All political entities, whether states, corporations, organizations, or individuals, are subjects of Imperium. Moreover, sovereignty has been redefined. Rather than involving a state's protection against aggression by others and assertions of a monopoly of law and violence within the national territory, sovereignty has now become a state's obligation to protect the global system from those who would disrupt it. The regulatory and legal framework of this "new sovereignty" is, of course, a good deal more complicated. Because Imperium is substantially economic, globalized regulations, such as those of the World Trade Organization, specify those practices that are required and those that are forbidden, both of which are meant to "stabilize" the system.[18]

Those states that refuse to accept Imperium's regulations or to acknowledge its *diktats* are subject to "regime change." Saddam Hussein's refusal to follow the rules laid down by Washington was not so much a threat to global security as a challenge to the foundations of Imperium; the same may yet prove to be the case with Iran. North Korea's willingness to yield to Imperium, in the final analysis, is not a matter of negotiation but of coercion. The American executive branch, acting in the role of Imperium's center, reserves the right to decide what constitutes an acceptable and legitimate government and to change those regimes that are not. As articulated in the *National Security Strategy* of 2002, "In building a balance of power that favors freedom, the United States is guided by the conviction that all nations have important responsibilities. Nations that enjoy freedom must actively fight terror. Nations that depend on international stability must help prevent the spread of weapons of mass destruction. Nations that seek international aid must govern themselves wisely, so that aid is well spent. For freedom to thrive, accountability must be expected and required" (p. iv). Whether states are being sufficiently accountable depends on the judgment of Imperium.[19]

There are two audiences that must be convinced of the legitimacy and legality of the Constitution of Imperium. The first is the American domestic polity, including Congress, the courts, and the public. Are the U.S. Constitution and statutory law being violated when the sovereign acts contrary to them? For that matter, *is* there a sovereign, and who *is* the sovereign? President Bush and the Justice Department lawyers (among others) argue that Congress, by dint of its resolution supporting any and all action necessary to capture and put an end to the activities of those responsible for the 9/11 attacks, has essentially acknowledged the sovereign power and authority of the executive branch. Thus, the president may do whatever is required, and whatever is required is constitutional (in contradistinction to Schmitt's argument). Extending this logic, President Bush is not only within his rights to order such seemingly unconstitutional actions as secret wiretapping, incarceration of "unlawful enemy combatants" without habeas corpus, and even extreme interrogation techniques. As sovereign, he is also within his rights to arrest the judiciary and disband Congress, should they challenge him and thereby "threaten national security." This he has not attempted to do, or even suggested, although the vitriol directed against "liberal" and "traitorous" judges, senators, and representatives has almost certainly been intended to mute, if not suppress, such dissent. We might also presume that a president would recognize the possibility of impeachment, should he make any too-aggressive moves to constrain or overrule the other two branches of the government—the behavior of Congress and courts notwithstanding. No doubt there are plans hidden somewhere in secure safes, on land, sea, and air, that specify procedures to be followed in the event of such circumstances.[20]

The international audience is in many ways both less important and more. Its members can never be citizens of Imperium, even though they are its subjects. On the one hand, the Bush administration's contempt for international law and institutions is only too clear: Those treaties and organizations that limit America's freedom to act in its own interests represent undesirable and illegal limits on U.S. sovereignty. On the other hand, the administration also desires approval, legitimation, and legalization of its actions, including those that undermine international law. Thus, it can claim not only that it is not in violation of that law but also that it is, in fact, upholding that law for the benefit of the world's states and people. Here language and rhetoric become centrally important; judges, lawyers, and scholars carry little weight in the face of public opinion, media frenzies, and what can only be called the "Big Lie." The effectiveness of the last is visible in the continuing belief among half of the U.S. public as recently as 2007 that the Iraqi regime of Saddam Hussein was involved in the attacks of 9/11 and in the administration's continuing effort to make that connection, albeit in more and more convoluted ways. As President Bush so eloquently put it on August 21, 2006: "Nobody's ever suggested that the attacks of September the 11th were ordered by Iraq. I have suggested, however, that resentment and the lack of hope create the breeding grounds for terrorists who are willing to use suiciders [sic] to kill . . . [where there was] so much resentment and so much hatred that people came and killed 3,000 of our citizens."[21]

We might doubt that the international audience is quite so convinced of this connection, but that matters less than the broad and gradual acquiescence and conditioning to Imperium's unilateralism and power. The UN Security Council refused to approve the U.S.-led invasion of Iraq, yet the United Nations and various member countries are now deeply involved in reconstruction and pacification efforts in Iraq. It may even fall to the UN to take over in Iraq. By creating conditions on the ground, the United States has forced its allies and the United Nations to become involved in what was a clear violation of international law yet has subsequently begun to acquire the veneer of instrumental legality. (How else can the United States and Britain be described as the legal "occupying powers" in Iraq?) Should Bush's successor in the White House decide to back off on some of the more egregious acts and claims of the current administration, the rest of the world will breathe a sigh of relief. Yet at the same time the world will almost surely accept many of the former administration's once-illegal policies, even if they continue to constitute technical violations of international law.

Chapter Eight

Twilight

And what of the future? As I write in early 2008, there is some doubt that Imperium will or can be sustained in its current form, especially given the uncertain future of the U.S. occupation of Iraq, the manifest failures of the global war on terror (GWOT), and growing uncertainties in global securities and credit markets. The mounting costs of the first war, the rising death toll, and widespread and growing disillusionment and disgust with the Bush administration, not to mention an impending presidential election, have generated numerous attacks on American unilateralism from commentators on both the right—which thinks the project has been botched but might yet be a success—and left—most of whom agree with the Right on the first point and some of whom believe the second, too. Others on the left (and a very few on the right) continue to think the entire project a disaster from the start. Both seem to fear that the era of U.S. hegemony may be almost over and that a resulting loss of credibility and power will expose the world to constant depredation by terrorists.[1]

These views, I would suggest, read too much into the excessive idealism of the neoconservative project of a "new Middle

East" and too little into the historical sociology of Imperium, the foundations of which were established at the end of World War II, and which is much less dependent on the overt exercise of military force than is widely assumed. The problematic relationship among state, citizen, and Imperium will not go away simply because George W. Bush leaves the White House or U.S. troops leave Iraq. To be sure, given current uncertainties in financial markets, Imperium's global political economy could collapse, returning the world to some *doppelgänger* of the 1930s, with its blocs in conflict. It is much more probable that, with a few hitches and hiccups, the next president of the United States will sustain some version of Imperium, which is neither global market nor global state, but a curious and largely unexamined hybrid of public power and private wealth.[2]

It is in this light that most work on empire and imperialism falls short, as a result of failures in both historical interpretation and sociological explanation. In particular, I suggest that, notwithstanding the literary and analytical force of much of their work, Michael Hardt and Antonio Negri have largely ignored history in their historical materialism and have also failed to analyze the institutional aspects of their empire. Both of these points bear consideration. For the first, I maintain that the world is in a period of transition, and not only from Fordism to post-Fordism and material to intellectual production and consumption, as it is usually stylized. Contemporary globalization is also linked to a fairly radical transformation in the very nature of property rights, which are so central and fundamental to capitalism. This transformation is taking place at all levels—global, national, individual—and, although it does not represent a complete break with what came before, it might be as important as the shift that took place during the transition from feudalism to capitalism in England between 1300 and 1700.[3]

For the second, we must recognize that there are certain foundational beliefs and practices that underpin the rules and relations of international politics as it has developed over the past half millennium and the past sixty years. Although from the perspective of the specialist in international relations nothing seems to have changed since Thucydides composed *The Peloponnesian War*—states continue to confront states under conditions of only marginally moderated anarchy—there are different forms and degrees of anarchy. Global capitalism cannot combine its two basic requirements—stability of rules and high, risky returns through speculation—under conditions of unregulated anarchy in the market, a point made emphatically by Karl Polanyi in *The Great Transformation*. Although individual states might balance together against imperial powers, no one wants to kill the American golden goose. The stability of the global economy is under constant threat due to the absence of centralized political regulation—this was Polanyi's insight as well as that of the founders of Bretton Woods. Some kind of stable and legitimate arrangement offering political regulation of the global political economy is a must, if the system is not to decompose. This is not to argue that a world state is in the offing or that economic interdependence fosters relative peace; rather, it is to argue that most, if not all, of the world's wealthiest and most powerful countries, as well as many of the developing ones, have a strong interest in a stable regulatory arrangement that all can more or less support.[4]

All of this leads to what former Defense Secretary Donald Rumsfeld and others called the "long twilight struggle," referring, of course, to the GWOT, the fight with those who might seek to destroy the system, and the drive for American dominance, at least through the twenty-first century. This misconstrues the nature of the conflict, such as it is: The primary "struggle" is not about the possibility of system destruction, but rather over the rules, structures, and practices of world society. It is this latter struggle that will take a long time—and judging from human history, such struggles seem to be eternal in human politics. Moreover, there is more than one struggle underway these days.

On the one hand we may observe the struggle to centralize the regulation of world society, either through Imperium or some kind of multilateral global republic. On the other hand, we see that globalization also generates myriad struggles of opposition and resistance, for autonomy, independence, and the right and capacity to decide on the conditions governing political and social life. These are evident not only in global conflicts but also in many localized ones. In the North, for example, such conflicts are as diverse as the culture wars, the global justice movement, projects to "eat locally," and cultivation of "self-reliance." In the South, they take a broader range of forms, mostly aimed at similar goals but sometimes turning violent. An optimistic view would suggest that the two struggles for integration and diversity are not necessarily contradictory; the pessimistic view would say they cannot both succeed. But it helps not to be too teleological here; there is no obvious or necessary endpoint to history, and there is good reason to think that there will be much "muddling through" in the future.

If most work on Imperium and the future is flawed, do I have anything different to offer? To begin, I recapitulate some of the central points made throughout this book, and then offer some arguments. Empire is not a concept new to the United States. Throughout the nineteenth century, the expansion of the republic had an imperial connotation; *Westward the Course of Empire Takes Its Way* is the name of a famous painting hanging in the U.S. Capitol. Moreover, many imagined that, once reached, American expansion would not, could not stop at the Pacific Ocean's edge but would continue farther. Indeed, at the end of that century, having swallowed major portions of Mexico and more or less settled the issue of slavery, the United States began to go abroad in a serious political fashion, taking the Philippines, Cuba, and Puerto Rico and extending its economic tentacles throughout Latin America and into China. This is a well-known materialist history that tends to be downplayed in favor of ideals. After all, Woodrow Wilson and his successors tried to make the world "safe for democracy," not imperialism (even though the United States behaved very much like other imperial powers of the time).

Thus, according to this story, the United States eschewed imperial adventurism after World War II, pressuring its European allies to open access to their colonies and eventually to grant them independence. From a material perspective, however, there was more to this than a desire to see men and women free. The European empires were restricted economic zones, and the U.S. government and American businessmen believed that U.S. capital would be much more successful in penetrating weak, independent countries than better-defended empires. Harry Truman's "Point Four" and the whole panoply of economic development programs that followed were premised on such penetration. The result was more of a commercial empire than a strictly military or territorial one, although power was always there to be used, especially during the 1950s (as well as in the early years of the twenty-first century). The rhetoric of freedom, democracy, capitalism, and anticommunism, which always accompanied U.S. interventions in the Third World, seemed to deal more with the human mind than the human body and served to obscure the material nature of such commercial imperialism. Today the global economy remains central to the project of Imperium, but the events of the 1990s, and especially September 11, 2001, suggest that this economy cannot survive without making visible the sword, if not actually using it.

Several observations are apropos here. First, although economy is central to Imperium, Imperium is more than just the economy. Second, although economic imperialism may play a role in the extension of American power, economic imperialism is not the dominant feature of Imperium—rule is. And third, most of the impetus for Imperium has emerged from U.S. domestic politics and not, I would argue, some systemic imperative to expand or a global state incipient in U.S.-sponsored institutions. That is, empire has been immanent within U.S. foreign policy since at least the end of World War II, but it was politics within the United States, especially during the 1990s and since, that motivated the Bush administration to move so strongly in this direction. As is well known, the sources of the Bush administration's foreign policy are to be found in the draft of the 1992 *Defense Planning Guidance*, a document largely written by Paul Wolfowitz but not then adopted as policy. Other important elements included Protestant millennialism and the "revolution in military affairs." Together, the three formed a coalition of social forces able to construct a powerful conservative movement.[5]

During the 1990s the Wolfowitz plan was privatized, adopted, and expanded by members of the Project for the New American Century (PNAC), a cabal of neoconservative hawks, some of whom had been members of the Nixon and Reagan administrations, as well as others belonging to the other two factions of this Republican "social movement." They despised the Clinton administration, its failure to increase defense spending during the 1990s, and the absence of a grand strategic doctrine for permanent American dominance. In 1998 a group associated with PNAC—which included Donald Rumsfeld, Paul Wolfowitz, and Richard Perle, among others—sent a letter to Clinton warning him of the looming Iraqi threat and intending to expose the Democrats as "weak on defense," probably as a prelude to the presidential campaign then pending. In September 2000 PNAC issued a document called "Rebuilding America's Defenses," in which the authors wrote:

> At present the United States faces no global rival. America's grand strategy should aim to preserve and extend this advantageous position as far into the future as possible. There are, however, potentially powerful states dissatisfied with the current situation and eager to change it, if they can, in directions that endanger the relatively peaceful, prosperous and free condition the world enjoys today. Up to now, they have been deterred from doing so by the capability and global presence of American military power. But, as that power declines, relatively and absolutely, the happy conditions that follow from it will be inevitably undermined.

This document built quite explicitly upon Wolfowitz's 1992 draft, which was trashed after being leaked to the *New York Times*. Yet, like NSC-68, which was put aside by Harry Truman in early 1950 only to be retrieved after the outbreak of the Korean War in June of that year, PNAC's manifesto was given new life after September 11, 2001, and integrated into the 2002 *National Security Strategy,* a document breathtaking in both its objectives and hubris.[6]

The attacks on New York and Washington, D.C., did not really change anything, contrary to the conventional wisdom, and as I have argued in this book. They did, however, enable the Bush administration to declare a "state of exception," which made possible operationalization of the PNAC program and pursuit of Imperium. I do not mean to propose that there was an explicit plan or program to construct Imperium; there are active agents behind it, but what has resulted is more a consequence of happenstance, opportunism, and ahistorical policies. More critically, the potential failure of the military element does not mean failure of the project as a whole. Imperium may yet succeed, although not necessarily under American unilateralism or domination. Given the many challenges and tasks that face world society today, there are few alternatives to some kind of organized coordination among its many social components (not merely countries). That coordination will take a number of different and simultaneous forms, without any clearly definitive outcomes. The only thing we can be certain of is uncertainty itself.[7]

What *is* new and novel since 2001 is the Bush administration's Constitution of Imperium, a "charter" that offers rules that structure the "game" of global political economy. The most obvious of these structural rules is the U.S.-proclaimed unilateral right of preemptive intervention, as executed in Iraq and threatened against Iran. Although neither of these can be said to have been successful (so far), the very notion that military threats from others must be anticipated and eliminated *before* they develop, rather than being met and suppressed once manifest, goes far beyond the UN Charter's principles of self-defense. Yet this rule seems to be garnering some degree of support (so long as it is expressed in appropriate language), as is evident in tentative international support for preventing Iran and other "rogue states" from acquiring atomic weapons. Such gradual acquiescence, if not full acceptance, suggests the eventual institutionalization of a practice along the lines of a Great Power "right of intervention," especially on behalf of "human rights," albeit in some form that is not yet clear. No one is yet ready to transfer such capabilities wholesale to the United Nations or some other transnational police force; no country other than the United States has the capability at present to act in this way.[8]

The (perhaps temporary) establishment of a global system of taxation by the United States, albeit in the name of economy and security, also constitutes something of a new structural feature of Imperium. Other empires have, of course, taxed their subject territories and subjects and some, in doing so, have tumbled into bankruptcy. So far as I know, however, the current global dollar "overhang" is unique in its magnitude, if not in its originality. This monetarist strategy has emerged as a result of fiscal policies that, deliberate or not, have served to maximize American economic autonomy while deepening global dependence on the dollar; its origins are to be found in various ad hoc efforts to inject dollar liquidity into the international economy during the Cold War (loan to Britain, Marshall Plan, Truman Doctrine, Mutual Security Agency, etc.). As Fred Block pointed out thirty years ago, the Bretton Woods system was intended to undermine national capitalism and to put in place a more efficient accumulation mechanism based on transnational economies of scale. Eventually, modifications in these arrangements allowed the United States to finance its budget and trade deficits through massive borrowing abroad by, somewhat paradoxically, increasing the system's dependence on the relative stability of the dollar and institutionalizing the death grip that the issuer and holders of dollars have on each other.[9]

America's political and military strategies were constituted by, and in turn served to constitute, the economic system of the Cold War and today. Containment of the Soviet Union did not come cheaply, and financing the Cold War legitimized the export of not only goods and commodities to Europe and Japan, but also arms, men, and dollars. The Soviet invasion of Afghanistan in 1978, the Iran hostage crisis from 1979 to 1981, and the second Cold War (and, more recently, the GWOT) all served to justify large increases in military and security spending and unprecedented budget and current-account deficits. These served to dollarize the world further, even in the face of notional challenges by the yen and euro. None of this means that there were or are no threats to America's or the world's security. Rather, circumstances, conditions, and events that might have played out in different ways mark underdetermined historical inflection points at which different choices and actions became politically possible, all viewed through a specific Cold War lens. By contrast, the end of the Cold War, the collapse of the Soviet Union, and even the Gulf War of 1990–1991, which seemed to offer so much hope and opportunity, turned out to impose rather severe fiscal and strategic constraints on the Bush I and Clinton administrations. It was in part these constraints that gave voice to PNAC and its strategy for long-term American dominance, ready to be put into practice when the opportunity arose, as it eventually did on September 11, 2001.[10]

There are good reasons to think that in the coming years the United States will find itself unable to sustain Imperium in the highly unilateralist form pursued by the Bush administration. In this respect, the growing costs of the project, disaffection among allies, and deteriorating conditions in the Middle East all point toward greater moderation on the part of the next U.S. president, from whichever party he or she might hail. Moreover, the American experience in Iraq and Afghanistan suggests that the levels of military force permissible in such social warfare are nonetheless inadequate to the task of eliminating guerrilla-type oppositional forces (this was a lesson of the Vietnam War, in which Maxwell Taylor's notion of "flexible response" was put to the test and failed). The idea of "unconditional surrender" might have worked in World War II when, in pursuit of total victory, combatants were willing to commit the forces required to eliminate entire societies; it is no longer politically or militarily feasible today. Even diplomacy backed by force, a favorite of Madeleine Albright and the Clinton State Department, may only serve to increase intransigence among those being threatened or bombed.[11]

But even if the project of Imperium does not succeed in its present form, it will neither be wholly stripped of authority nor vanish, for institutions and practices do not always disappear, precedents are often left to stand, and people are always looking for things to do. It would be extremely disadvantageous for all concerned to allow the dollar to collapse and lose its role as the world's reserve currency. Not only would trillions of dollars in securities, bonds, and debt simply evaporate—as has already happened in the so-called subprime mortgage bubble and associated credit crisis—the resulting confusion and instability in global economic affairs would almost certainly lead to another Great Depression (although consider that even a 50 percent contraction in the size of the U.S. economy would still leave it the largest in the world). At some point, a rescue program for the dollar may become unavoidable and, however distasteful it might be, Europe, Japan, and China will have to step in to ensure that such a rescue succeeds. Imperium would be saved, although not in its unilateral American form.[12]

More important, perhaps, than global dollarization has been the intellectual property revolution led by the United States and the resulting disruption of social hierarchies over the past three decades. Some have called this "efficiency"; others see it as "enclosure of the global commons." The result has been and is likely to be generative of a good deal of social unrest and violence around the world. Most of the planet's elites have so far managed to land on their feet, but billions of others have been forced to jump without parachutes, as customary access to goods and property has been altered or lost without their approval or knowledge. The world's poorest seem unlikely to rise up collectively against this system, but in many countries middle-class social forces are increasingly disaffected as their social and economic prospects decline and political systems are denatured into a bland version of consumer choice. This disaffection manifests itself in different ways in different places, but it is mostly directed against the local representatives and manifestations of the American Imperium, even if such are European or Asian.[13]

The trajectory of Imperium may thus ultimately depend not on its ability to bring force and discipline to bear on the disaffected billions, but on the strength or weakness of its social base, which is wealthy but very much smaller than the rest of the world. In terms of sheer numbers, those whose well-being is tightly linked to the success of the global economy probably number no more than one billion. Their aggregate income might be on the order of $25 trillion, out of a global GDP of $35–40 trillion (and there is a lot of difference between Bill Gates and Joe Sixpack, notwithstanding their friendly drink in the same "tavern"). Among this billion, some number, while deeply interested in the world's future, are skeptical, dissenters, or on the margin. The remaining 5.5 billion of the world's people are economically important both locally and globally but constitute something of a *lumpenproletariat,* whose voice has been and will be denied by the better-off. They seem unlikely to organize or act unless some kind of mass middle-class movement leads them.[14]

Michael Hardt and Antonio Negri argue, rather idealistically and quite unrealistically, that a "multitude," consisting of those whose labor, both material and intellectual, is exploited by capital, and will eventually assert its power and bring an end to empire. As they put it: "We can imagine the day when the multitude will invent a weapon that will not only allow it to defend itself but will also be constructive, expansive, and constituent. It is not a matter of taking power and commanding the armies but destroying their very possibility." This outcome would seem to depend, however, on a broadly defined understanding of what constitutes labor under conditions of post-Fordist capitalism as well as the multitude's recognition that it is a "class in itself." There is a strong whiff of determinism and utopia about their argument, and both are problematic. Moreover, if my academic colleagues are included in the "multitude"—and they should be, given the knowledge-based nature of their work and their contract-based relationship with capital—such self-recognition is still far off. Margaret Thatcher famously pronounced that, "there is no alternative" (TINA), while the 2002 *National Security Strategy* pretentiously announced, ex cathedra, that, "The great struggles of the twentieth century between liberty and totalitarianism ended with a decisive victory for the forces of freedom—and a single sustainable model for national success: freedom, democracy, and free enterprise." To paraphrase Oliver Twist, "Is there any more?" Here, rather than falling back on history as do Hardt and Negri, it may be useful to fall back on historical parallels from the seventeenth and eighteenth centuries.[15]

The Bush administration's foreign policy is pitched in terms of a global war on those who violently oppose Imperium, but there are unmistakable elements of class and social struggle evident in the world that point to something different. Indeed, there is an interesting parallel between the rise of the absolutist state in Europe during the seventeenth and eighteenth centuries and Imperium today. Conventional historiography paints the conflicts of those past times in terms of coalitions of proto-democratic aristocrats and a rising bourgeoisie against tyrannical sovereigns who sought to crush all opposition. As Sandra Halperin has shown, the actual story is somewhat different: "European monarchs were concerned with undertaking a wide-ranging series of economic, fiscal, political, and social reforms: to improve agriculture, to encourage freer trade within their realms, to eliminate the privileges of religion and religious orders, to set up independent judiciaries, to substitute salaried officers for hereditary officeholders, and to improve the status of peasants. The landed and wealthy elite resisted every measure of reform and, throughout the [seventeenth] century, were at constant odds with royal administrations."

The efforts of the absolutist monarchs to bring the landed aristocracy and the towns and cities under state control were motivated by sovereigns' desire to reduce effective opposition as well as the need to generate revenues to pay for their own bureaucracies and armies. This was possible only if they could modernize the state and generate new sources of income.

According to Halperin, "One way of doing this was to extend market privileges to foreigners and to found cities with foreign and minority industrialists and commercial classes in order to obtain high ground rents and subjects capable of paying high taxes." The nationalist wars that followed during the nineteenth century were, she continues, a continuation of the class struggles of the eighteenth, representing efforts by social and economic elites to wrest control of the state from kings and queens and to reassert their local rights and privileges through exclusion of such privileged urban groups. That democratic systems eventually emerged from these struggles—and, for the most part, Halperin argues, this did not occur until *after* World War II—was quite unrelated to the state-building projects undertaken between 1600 and 1900.[16]

More to the point is the fact that many of those involved in the "secret societies" of prerevolutionary France, as well as the anti-imperial nationalist movements of the 1800s in other countries, were members of the bourgeois intelligentsia who organized against their exclusion from political life and, by extension, from the structural organization of the political economy. It is interesting to note how many professionals and professors occupied leadership positions in the Balkan Wars of the 1990s. Osama bin Laden and his lieutenants are by no means uneducated, either. When the middle classes allied with the aristocracy against the sovereign, the eventual settlement almost always bought off the wealthiest fraction of the bourgeoisie at the expense of the rest. Only when the middle class was able to build coalitions with the peasantry and working class was it possible to mount significant challenges to elite power structures.[17]

Today, much of the global bourgeoisie has bought into the benefits of neoliberal globalization, if not Imperium; such opposition as exists is directed against its military policy rather than its political economy. Conceptually, the links between Imperium's structuring of the global political economy and its military policies are poorly understood and not at all obvious, and the extraction of capital from the middle classes has been masked by a variety of fiscal ploys, such as tapping into home equities and other pools of "underexploited" money, such as pension funds. Short of nuclear war, today's elites are unlikely to be decimated as Europe's were during the twentieth century. But a global economic implosion that strips the world's middle class of its assets in a particularly brutal form of enclosure and deflation could have a social impact not too dissimilar from war. It could also trigger broad political mobilization across the globe.

In the global North, we might say, this revelation has yet to occur; not so, however, in many parts of the global South. There is no gainsaying that Imperium has generated considerable opposition around the world, although we might question whether such dissent is much of a threat to it. Still, *salafist jihadism* is not only a source of violence and terrorism, it is also a social movement whose support seems to be growing throughout the Muslim world and even in the West. The Egyptian Brotherhood, Hamas in Palestine, Hezbollah in Lebanon, and similar organizations elsewhere all provide social and welfare services that states and governments cannot afford to offer. Almost certainly these sorts of practices will be replicated in more and more places, and by more and more organizations, in the decades ahead. If Imperium is to survive, it will have to find ways to maintain middle-class support, provide public social goods to the impoverished, and diffuse oppositional forces. Can this be done? Will it be done?

It is too soon to tell.

Notes

1. According to J. R. Richardson, "Imperium Romanum: Empire and the Language of Power," *Journal of Roman Studies* 81 (1991): 1–9: "Only magistrates proposed *leges* [legislation] and were responsible for jurisdiction; only magistrates and pro-magistrates were able, through their Imperium, to command" (p. 2).

Chapter 1

1. As explained later, I use the term "Imperium" rather than "empire" to denote the nature of command through rules and rule rather than control of territories outside the imperial core; see Nicholas G. Onuf, *World of Our Making: Rules and Rule in Social Theory and International Relations* (Columbia: University of South Carolina Press, 1989).

2. By now the literature on "empire" is vast. Among the sources I have found most thought provoking are the two volumes by Michael Hardt and Antonio Negri, *Empire* (Cambridge, Mass.: Harvard University Press, 2000) and *Multitude—War and Democracy in the Age of Empire* (New York: Penguin Press, 2004); although not read until after this book was substantially completed, Charles S. Maier, *Among Empires—American Ascendancy and Its Predecessors* (Cambridge, Mass.: Harvard University Press, 2006); and Andrew J. Bacevich, *American Empire—The Realities and Consequences of U.S. Diplomacy* (Cambridge, Mass.: Harvard University Press, 2002). On the more general question of empire, see G. John Ikenberry, "Illusions of Empire: Defining the New American

Order," *Foreign Affairs* 83, 2 (March/April 2004): 144–156. Also useful have been Ugo Mattei, "A Theory of Imperial Law: A Study on U.S. Hegemony and the Latin Resistance," *Global Jurist Frontiers* 3, 2 (2003): article 1, www.bepress.com/gj/frontiers/vol3/iss2/art1/ (accessed March 30, 2005); and Hauke Brunkhorst, "The Right to War: Hegemonial Geopolitics or Civic Constitutionalism," *Constellations* 11, 4 (2004): 512–526. Other sources can be found in the following notes and on the Global Policy Forum's Web site on "Empire?": www.global policy.org/empire/index.htm (accessed November 15, 2007).

3. These are, of course, among the arguments made by Hardt and Negri in *Empire*. See also Maier, *Among Empires*, especially chapters 5–6. On CIA activities, see Jane Mayer, "The Black Sites," *New Yorker*, August 13, 2007, www.newyorker.com/reporting/2007/08/13/070 813fa_fact_mayer (accessed September 26, 2007). On Bush's comments, see George W. Bush, "President Discusses Creation of Military Commissions to Try Suspected Terrorists," The White House, Office of the Press Secretary, September 6, 2006, www.whitehouse.gov/news/releases/2006/09/20060906-3.html (accessed September 6, 2006). On the "sole organ," see Louis Fisher, "The 'Sole Organ' Doctrine," *The Law Library of Congress,* August 2006 (2006-03236), www.fas.org/sgp/eprint/fisher.pdf (accessed September 26, 2007). On the assertion of executive authority, see Frederick A. O. Schwartz Jr. and Aziz Z. Huq, *Unchecked and Unbalanced—Presidential Power in a Time of Terror* (New York: The New Press, 2007); and Charlie Savage, *Takeover—The Return of the Imperial Presidency and the Subversion of American Democracy* (New York: Little, Brown, 2007).

4. Carl Schmitt, *Political Theology: Four Chapters on the Concept of Sovereignty* (Cambridge, Mass.: MIT Press, 1965). Quote is on page 6. On Schmitt, see also Jef Huysmans, "International Politics of Insecurity: Normativity, Inwardness and the Exception," *Security Dialogue* 37, 1 (March 2006): 11–29; and Roland Axtmann, "Humanity or Enmity? Carl Schmitt on International Politics," *International Politics* 44, 5 (September 2007): 531–551.

5. John Yoo has been reported as having said, in 2002, "What the administration is trying to do is create a new legal regime," although he was not specific about the scope of that regime; see Warren Richeym "How Long Can Guantanamo Prisoners Be Held?" *The Christian Science Monitor,* April 9, 2002, at http://www.csmonitor .com/2002/0409/p01s03-usju.html (accessed March 24, 2008); and John Yoo, "The Changing Laws of War: Do We Need a New Legal Regime after September 11?" *Notre Dame Law Review* 79 (July 2004): 1183–1235. The president did order the Justice Department to prepare

an assessment of his legal authority; he did not, however, seek at that point to extend his authority beyond the territory of the United States or to imagine Imperium into existence. The internal debates are recounted by Bob Woodward in *Bush at War* (New York: Simon & Schuster, 2002) and its sequels. The war in Afghanistan is addressed in Steve Coll, *Ghost Wars: The Secret History of the CIA, Afghanistan, and Bin Laden, from the Soviet Invasion to September 10, 2001* (New York: Penguin, 2004).

6. On Addington, see Jane Mayer, "The Hidden Power," *The New Yorker,* July 3, 2006, www.newyorker.com/archive/2006/07/03 /060703fa_fact1 (accessed September 26, 2007); and Jack L. Goldsmith, *The Terror Presidency—Law and Judgment Inside the Bush Administration* (New York: Norton, 2007). About Yoo, the Boalt Hall Web site notes, somewhat dryly, that, "From 2001 to 2003, he served as a deputy assistant attorney general in the Office of Legal Counsel at the U.S. Department of Justice, where he worked on issues involving foreign affairs, national security and the separation of powers." See www.law .berkeley.edu/faculty/profiles/facultyProfile.php?facID=235 (accessed June 9, 2006). As Anne-Marie Slaughter has written about the invasion of Iraq, "by giving up on the Security Council, the Bush Administration has started on a course that could be called 'illegal but legitimate.'" "Good Reasons for Going Around the UN," *New York Times,* March 18, 2003, http://query.nytimes.com/gst/fullpage.html?res=9E0CEFD D1431F93BA25750C0A9659C8B63 (accessed September 26, 2007). Slaughter is cited in an article by Anne Orford that addresses more broadly the question of who "transcends the law and thus assures its meaning and its enforcement" and asks the provocative and thought-provoking question, "what lies beyond the UN Charter[?]"; "The Destiny of International Law," *Leiden Journal of International Law* 17 (2004): 441–476, cites on pp. 444, 441. On lawyers' need to legalize everything, see Robert Granfield, "Lawyers and Power: Reproduction and Resistance in the Legal Profession," *Law & Society Review* 30, 1 (1996): 205–223, especially pp. 207–211. On unwritten constitutions, see Judith Pryor, "Unwritten Constitutions?" *European Journal of English Studies* 11, 1 (2007): 79–92.

7. On the histories of empires, see, e.g., Susan E. Alcock et al., eds., *Empires—Perspectives from Archaeology and History* (Cambridge, England: Cambridge University Press, 2001); Eric Hobsbawm, *The Age of Empire, 1875–1914* (New York: Vintage, 1989); Jennifer Pitts, *A Turn to Empire—The Rise of Imperial Liberalism in Britain and France* (Princeton, N.J.: Princeton University Press, 2005); Niall Ferguson, *Empire: The Rise*

and Demise of the British World Order and the Lessons for Global Power (New York: Basic, 2004); and Niall Ferguson, *Colossus—The Rise and Fall of the American Empire* (New York: Penguin, 2005). On similarities and differences, see William Appleman Williams, *Empire as a Way of Life* (New York: Oxford University Press, 1980); Sebastian Mallaby, "The Reluctant Imperialist: Terrorism, Failed States, and the Case for American Empire," *Foreign Affairs* 81, 2 (March/April 2002); Maier, *Among Empires;* and Bacevich, *American Empire.* On the benefits of empire, see Robert Kagan, *Of Paradise and Power—America and Europe in the New World Order* (New York: Knopf, 2003); Dinesh D'Souza, "In Praise of American Empire," *Christian Science Monitor,* April 26, 2002, www.csmonitor.com/2002/0426/p11s01-coop.html (accessed November 24, 2003); and Deepak Lal, *In Defense of Empires* (Washington, D.C.: AEI Press, 2004), www.aei.org/docLib/20040902_book790text.pdf (accessed July 10, 2005). On the evil and aggressive nature of American empire, see Chalmers Johnson, *The Sorrows of Empire—Militarism, Secrecy, and the End of the Republic* (New York: Metropolitan Books, 2004). On the determinist nature of expansion, see Robert Jervis, "The Compulsive Empire," *Foreign Policy* 137 (July/August 2003): 82–87.

8. One version of the logic of empire can be found in Ivo H. Daalder and James M. Lindsay, *America Unbound—The Bush Revolution in Foreign Policy* (Washington, D.C.: Brookings Institution Press, 2003). On the ad hoc decision-making process, see Michel Foucault, "Nietzsche, Genealogy, History," in *The Essential Foucault,* ed. Paul Rabinow and Nikolas Rose, 351–369 (New York: The New Press, 2003). In Foucault's words, "Genealogy does not resemble the evolution of a species and does not map the destiny of a people. On the contrary, to follow the complex course of descent is to maintain passing events in their proper dispersion; it is to identify the accidents, the minute deviations—or conversely, the complete reversals—the errors, the false appraisals, and the faulty calculations that gave birth to those things which to continue to exist and have value for us; it is to discover that truth or being lies not at the root of what we know and what we are but the exteriority of accidents" (p. 355). See also Max Weber, "Bureaucracy," *Wirtschaft und Gesellschaft,* part III, ch. 6, 650–678, cited in *From Max Weber: Essays in Sociology,* ed. and trans. H. H. Gerth and C. Wright Mills, 280 (New York: Oxford University Press, 1946). On the role of contingency, see Stephen J. Gould, *Wonderful Life: Burgess Shale and the Nature of History* (New York: Norton, 1989). Some scholars, such as William Appleman Williams (*Empire as a Way of Life*), have argued that

empire was already codified in the U.S. Constitution at its ratification and was perpetrated and perpetuated by elites fearful of the political and social consequences of territorial limits.

9. Ronnie D. Lipschutz, *After Authority—War, Peace and Global Politics in the 21st Century* (Albany: State University of New York Press, 2000); Ronnie D. Lipschutz, "The Clash of Governmentalities: The Fall of the UN Republic and America's Reach for Imperium," *Contemporary Security Policy* 23, 2 (December 2002): 214–231; Ronnie D. Lipschutz, "From 'Culture Wars' to Shooting Wars: Cultural Conflict in the United States," in *The Myth of "Ethnic" Conflict: Politics, Economics, and "Cultural" Violence,"* ed. Beverly Crawford and Ronnie D. Lipschutz, 394–433 (Berkeley: University of California–Berkeley Institute of Area Studies Press, 1998); Ronnie D. Lipschutz, "Capitalism, Conflict and Churn: How the American Culture War Went Global," in *World Cultures Yearbook 2007: Cultures, Conflict and Globalization,* ed. H. Anheier and Y. R. Isar, 185–196 (London: Sage, 2007); Ronnie D. Lipschutz, "Introduction," *Civil Societies and Social Movements: Domestic, Transnational, Global,* ed. Ronnie D. Lipschutz, xi–xxviii (Aldershot, Hampshire: Ashgate Publishing, 2006).

10. The 9/11 Commission, *Final Report of the National Commission on Terrorist Attacks upon the United States* (New York: Norton, 2004), 362. On the relationship of domestic politics and foreign policy, see Kiron K. Skinner, Serhiy Kudelia, Bruce Bueno de Mesquita, and Condoleezza Rice, "Politics Starts at the Water's Edge," *New York Times,* September 15, 2007, www.nytimes.com/2007/09/15/opinion/15skin ner.html (accessed September 17, 2007); and Bacevich, *American Empire.* On FBI offices abroad, see Office of the Inspector General, "Federal Bureau of Investigation Legal Attaché Program," Report No. 04–18, March 2004, www.usdoj.gov/oig/reports/FBI/a0418/chap1 .htm (accessed December 20, 2007).

11. On the postwar period, see Clinton Rossiter, *Constitutional Dictatorship—Crisis Government in the Modern Democracies* (Princeton, N.J.: Princeton University Press, 1948). On nuclear terrorism, see Howard D. Russell and James J. F. Forest, *Weapons of Mass Destruction and Terrorism* (Columbus, Ohio: McGraw-Hill, 2008); and Graham Allison, *Nuclear Terrorism: The Ultimate Preventable Catastrophe* (New York: Times Books, 2004).

12. See Maier, *Among Empires*; Michael Hudson, *Super Imperialism—The Origin and Fundamentals of U.S. World Dominance,* 2nd ed. (London: Pluto Press, 2003); and Peter Gowan, *The Global Gamble—Washington's Faustian Bid for World Dominance* (London: Verso, 1999).

13. Daniel C. Thomas, *The Helsinki Effect: International Norms, Human Rights and the Demise of Communism* (Princeton, N.J.: Princeton University Press, 2001); and Margaret E. Keck and Kathryn Sikkink, *Activists Beyond Borders—Advocacy Networks in International Politics* (Ithaca, N.Y.: Cornell University Press, 1998). On what is "beyond international law," see Orford, "The Destiny of International Law."

14. In fact, an Internet search suggests that it is none too clear who asked the question—Andre Malraux, Archduke Otto von Habsburg, and Kissinger are all cited—or when it was asked—1953, 1971—or whether it was Zhou or Mao Zedong who offered the famous reply.

Chapter 2

1. On the global state, power, and authority, see Martin Shaw, *Theory of the Global State: Globality as an Unfinished Revolution* (Cambridge, England: Cambridge University Press, 2000); and Michael Barnett and Raymond Duvall, *Power and Global Governance* (Cambridge, England: Cambridge University Press, 2005). On the possibility of a world state, see Alex Wendt, "Why a World State Is Inevitable," *European Journal of International Affairs* 9, 4 (2003): 491–542; and Charles S. Maier, *Among Empires—American Ascendancy and Its Predecessors* (Cambridge, Mass.: Harvard University Press, 2006).

2. Michel Foucault, "Governmentality," in *The Essential Foucault* ed. Paul Rabinow and Nikolas Rose, 229–245 (New York: The New Press, 2003); see also Mitchell Dean, *Governmentality: Power and Rule in Modern Society* (London: Sage, 1999). On the rejection of multilateralism, see, e.g., John M. Broder, "Bush Outlines Proposal on Climate Change," *New York Times*, September 28, 2007, www.nytimes.com /2007/09/28/world/28cnd-climate.html?hp (accessed September 28, 2007); and David Harvey, *A Brief History of Neoliberalism* (Oxford: Oxford University Press, 2005). On the follies of the self-regulating market, see Karl Polanyi, *The Great Transformation* (Boston: Beacon, 1944, 1957, 2000). The failures of underregulated markets are now only too evident in the developing global economic situation.

3. On the economic origins of Imperium, see Fred L. Block, *The Origins of International Economic Disorder* (Berkeley: University of California Press, 1977); Michael Hudson, *Super Imperialism—The Origin and Fundamentals of U.S. World Dominance,* 2nd ed. (London: Pluto Press, 2003); and Peter Gowan, *The Global Gamble—Washington's Faustian Bid*

for World Dominance (London: Verso, 1999). On the theological sources of U.S. foreign policy, see Anatole Lieven, *America Right or Wrong—An Anatomy of American Nationalism* (Oxford: Oxford University Press, 2004); on the parallels between neoconservative and millennial teleologies, see Michael Northcott, *An Angel Directs the Storm—Apocalyptic Religion and American Empire* (London: I.B. Tauris, 2004); and Christopher Collins, *Homeland Mythology—Biblical Narratives in American Culture* (University Park: Penn State Press, 2007). The teleological quality of the West's "triumph" is well-expressed in Francis Fukuyama, *The End of History and the Last Man* (New York: Free Press, 1992). Anthony Lake, Bill Clinton's national security adviser, seems to have coined the term "enlargement"—which to me always sounded rather painful—to describe the process of teleological expansion that was later codified as the "Washington Consensus." See Remarks of Anthony Lake, Assistant to the President for National Security Affairs, "From Containment to Enlargement," Johns Hopkins University School of Advanced International Studies, Washington, D.C., September 21, 1993, www.mtholyoke.edu/acad/intrel/lakedoc.html (accessed September 28, 2007). Finally, the invasion of Iraq was offered as necessary to creation of "the New Middle East," that part of the world in which the battle of Armageddon and the return of Christ are meant to occur (albeit with considerable disagreement among believers about the precise circumstances and whether human intervention can hasten the millennium).

4. On the conventional story, see John Lewis Gaddis, *The Cold War—A New History* (New York: Penguin, 2005); and Condoleezza Rice, "Promoting the National Interest," *Foreign Affairs* 79, 1 (January/February 2000): 45–62. On the supposed role of Ronald Reagan in the ending of the Cold War, see Peter Schweizer, *Victory: The Reagan Administration's Secret Strategy That Hastened the Collapse of the Soviet Union* (Boston: Atlantic Monthly Press, 1996); and Peter Schweizer, *Reagan's War: The Epic Story of His Forty-Year Struggle and Final Triumph over Communism* (New York: Anchor, 2003). On wartime planning for the postwar period, see Laurence H. Shoup and William Minter, *Imperial Brain Trust: The Council on Foreign Relations and United States Foreign Policy* (New York: Monthly Review Press, 1977).

5. Paul Johnson, "From the Evil Empire to the Empire for Liberty," *The New Criterion* 21, 10 (June 2003), http://newcriterion.com:81/archive/21/jun03/johnson.htm (accessed September 28, 2007); William Appleman Williams, *Empire as a Way of Life* (New York: Oxford University Press, 1980); Max Boot, "Neither New nor Nefarious: The Liberal Empire Strikes Back," *Current History* 101, 658 (November 2003): 361–366, www.currenthistory.com/org_pdf,

_files/102/667/102_667_361.pdf (accessed September 28, 2007); and Michael Hunt, *Ideology and U.S. Foreign Policy* (New Haven, Conn.: Yale University Press, 1987). A recent discussion of the Open Door can be found in Christopher Layne, *The Peace of Illusions—American Grand Strategy from 1940 to the Present* (Ithaca, N.Y.: Cornell University Press, 2007), ch. 4.

6. According to the Atlantic Charter, signed on August 14, 1941, "The President of the United States of America and the Prime Minister, Mr. Churchill, representing His Majesty's Government in the United Kingdom, being met together, deem it right to make known certain common principles in the national policies of their respective countries on which they base their hopes for a better future for the world....Third, they respect the right of all peoples to choose the form of government under which they will live; and they wish to see sovereign rights and self government restored to those who have been forcibly deprived of them," www.yale.edu/lawweb/avalon/wwii/atlantic.htm (accessed December 20, 2007). On dealing with weak countries rather than strong empires, see Sidney Lens, *The Forging of the American Empire* (London: Pluto, 2003), ch. 16. On triangular trade, see Arthur R. Upgren, "Triangular Trade," *Journal of Political Economy* 43, 5 (October 1935): 653–673; and Albert O. Hirschman, *National Power and the Structure of Foreign Trade* (Berkeley: University of California Press, 1935). On relations with postcolonial countries, see, e.g., Gabriel Kolko, *Confronting the Third World* (New York: Pantheon, 1988).

7. On "soft empire," see Joseph S. Nye Jr., *Soft Power—The Means to Success in World Politics* (New York: Public Affairs, 2004). Niall Ferguson cobbles together quotes from Harry S Truman to attribute to him the argument that, "The only way to 'save the world from totalitarianism . . .' was for 'the whole world [to] adopt the American system'" (*Colossus—The Rise and Fall of the American Empire* [New York: Penguin, 2005], p. 80). On the apparent virtues of the American way, see Louis Hartz, *The Liberal Tradition in America* (New York: Harcourt Brace, 1955); and Albert O. Hirschman, *The Passion and the Interests: Political Arguments for Capitalism before Its Triumph* (Princeton, N.J.: Princeton University Press). On the successes and failures of development theory, see Gilbert Rist, *The History of Development—from Western Origins to Global Faith,* new ed. (London: Zed, 2002). Recently there has been considerable excitement about the reduction of global poverty; the percentage of the world's people living on less than $2 a day has dropped from some 44 percent in 1980 to about 18 percent today—with most of the change in China and India. That still leaves the world with approximately 1.2 billion impoverished people. See Xavier Sala-

i-Martin, "The Disturbing 'Rise' of Global Income Inequality," National Bureau of Economic Research, Washington, D.C., Working Paper 8904, www.nber.org/papers/W8904 (accessed October 5, 2007).

8. Block, *Origins of International Economic Disorder*; and Maier, *Among Empires*. Import substitution strategies worked, but they impose high costs on consumers, thereby restraining growth and sometimes preventing foreign investors from exporting profits. The standard examples of economic success are Japan, South Korea, Taiwan, and, most recently, the People's Republic of China, all of which were allowed to export into the U.S. market, which absorbed their surplus production. See Bruce Cumings, "The Origins and Development of the Northeast Asian Political Economy," *International Organization* 38 (1984): 1–40. Economic crises in Mexico are an example of pressures on the middle class, but this has happened in many other countries. On Iran, see Mark J. Gasiorowski and Malcolm Byrne, eds. *Mohammad Mosaddeq and the 1953 Coup in Iran* (Syracuse, N.Y.: Syracuse University Press, 2004); and Mark J. Gasiorowski, *U.S. Foreign Policy and the Shah: Building a Client State in Iran* (Ithaca, N.Y.: Cornell University Press, 1991). On developing countries' resistance to foreign pressures, see Stephen D. Krasner, *Structural Conflict—The Third World Against Global Liberalism* (Berkeley: University of California Press, 1985); and Ronnie D. Lipschutz, *When Nations Clash—Raw Materials, Ideology and Foreign Policy* (New York: Harper/Ballinger, 1989).

9. On the difficulty of maintaining a technological edge, see Shelley Hurt, "Science, Power, and the State: U.S. Foreign Policy, Intellectual Property Law, and the Origins of the World Trade Organization, 1969–1994" (PhD diss., Department of Political Science, The New School for Social Research, 2008). John G. Ruggie, viewing this program through a more benign lens, described it as "embedded liberalism." See the following articles and chapters by Ruggie: "International Regimes, Transactions and Change: Embedded Liberalism in the Postwar Economic Order," in *International Regimes,* ed. Stephen D. Krasner, 195–232 (Ithaca, N.Y.: Cornell University Press, 1983); "Embedded Liberalism Revisited: Institution and Progress in International Economic Relations," in *Progress in International Relations,* ed. Emmanuel Adler and Beverly Crawford, 201–234 (New York: Columbia University Press, 1991); "At Home Abroad, Abroad at Home: International Liberalisation and Domestic Stability in the New World Economy," *Millennium* 24, 3 (Winter 1995): 507–526; and "Taking Embedded Liberalism Global: The Corporate Connection," 2003, www.law.nyu.edu/kingsburyb/spring03/globalization/ruggiepaper.pdf (accessed March 10, 2004). As a group of oil company representatives told U.S. Secre-

tary of State Dean Acheson in 1951, they were concerned about "the very grave consequences of giving the Iranians terms more favorable than other countries. They expressed the opinion that if this were done the entire international oil industry would be seriously threatened. The opinion was offered that even the loss of Iran would be preferable to the instability which would be created by making too favorable an agreement with Iran." Cited in Lipschutz, *When Nations Clash*, 59. See also Kolko, *Confronting the Third World*; and Jonathan Kwitny, *Endless Enemies—The Making of an Unfriendly World* (New York: Penguin, 1986).

10. Peter B. Kenen, ed., *Managing the World Economy—Fifty Years after Bretton Woods* (Washington, D.C.: Institute for International Economics, 1994); Block, *Origins of International Economic Disorder*; and James R. O'Connor, *The Fiscal Crisis of the State* (New York: St. Martin's Press, 1973).

11. Hudson, *Super Imperialism*; Jonathan Nitzan and Shimshon Bichler, "Capitalism and War," *Tikkun*, August 9, 2006, http://bn archives.yorku.ca/205/02/20060809nb_cheap_wars.pdf (accessed December 19, 2007); Martin Feldstein, "The Underfunded Pentagon," *Foreign Affairs* 86, 2 (March/April, 2007); David Gold, "Does Military Spending Stimulate or Retard Economic Performance? Revisiting an Old Debate," New School University, International Affairs Working Paper 2005–01, January 2005, www.nsu.newschool.edu/international affairs/docs/wkg_papers/Gold_2005–01.pdf (accessed December 19, 2007); and Andrew D. James, "U.S. Defence R&D Spending: An Analysis of the Impacts—Rapporteur's Report for the EURAB Working Group ERA Scope and Vision" (PREST, University of Manchester, UK, January 2004), http://ec.europa.eu/research/eurab/pdf/recom mendations10.pdf (accessed December 19, 2007).

12. Joanne Gowa, *Closing the Gold Window—Domestic Politics and the End of Bretton Woods* (Ithaca, N.Y.: Cornell University Press, 1983). The Eurodollar market emerged as one means of absorbing the dollar glut, but it seems to have only encouraged the United States to export even more dollars.

13. This, of course, is the dilemma faced by China, Japan, and Europe today: to hold dollars or to dump them. See John Ralston Saul, *The Collapse of Globalism and the Reinvention of the World* (London: Atlantic Books, 2005); and Hudson, *Super Imperialism*. I return to the contemporary "dollar dilemma" in later chapters. On the origins of fiscal discipline, see Mark D. Harmon, *The British Labour Government and the 1976 IMF Crisis* (Houndmills, Basingstoke, UK: Macmillan, 1997).

14. On the military-political-economic strategies of the Nixon administration, see Maier, *Among Empires*. On interdependence, see,

e.g., Henry A. Kissinger, U.S. Secretary of State, "A New National Part-nership" (speech, Los Angeles, January 24, 1975), cited in Robert O. Keohane and Joseph S. Nye, *Power and Interdependence: World Politics in Transition* (Boston: Little, Brown, 1977); and Robert Gilpin, *U.S. Power and the Multinational Corporation* (New York: Basic, 1975). SDRs still exist but represent units of account rather than international liquidity; see www.imf.org/external/np/exr/facts/sdr.HTM (accessed August 15, 2007).

15. On the rise of the neoconservatives, see Jerry W. Sanders, *Ped-dlers of Crisis: The Committee on the Present Danger and the Legitimation of Containment Militarism in the Korean Wars and Post-Vietnam Periods* (Boston: South End Press, 1983); and Norman Podhoretz, *The Present Danger: Do We Have the Will to Reverse the Decline of American Power?* (New York: Simon & Schuster, 1980). On the Christian Right, see Leo P. Ribuffo, *The Old Christian Right—The Protestant Far Right from the Great Depression to the Cold War* (Philadelphia: Temple University Press, 1983), 259–274. On the "resource war," see Galen Spencer Hull, *Pawns on a Chessboard: The Resource War in Southern Africa* (Washington, D.C.: University Press of America, 1981); Galen Spencer Hull, "The Possibil-ity of a Resource War in Southern Africa," testimony before the House Subcommittee on Africa of the Committee on Foreign Affairs, 97th Cong., 1st sess. July 8, 1981 (Washington, D.C.: U.S. Government Printing Office, 1981); and the citations in Lipschutz, *When Nations Clash*. On the winning coalition in 1980, see Jack W. Germond and Jules Witcover, *Blue Smoke and Mirrors: How Reagan Won and Why Carter Lost the Election of 1980* (New York: Viking, 1981).

16. Paul Kengor, *God and Ronald Reagan: A Spiritual Life* (New York: Regan Books, 2004); Steve Bruce, *Conservative Protestant Politics* (Oxford: Oxford University Press, 1998), ch. 5; and Mark Gerson, *The Neoconservative Vision—From the Cold War to the Culture Wars* (Lanham, Md.: Madison Books, 1996).

17. On the Reagan economic strategy and budget problems, see Gowan, *The Global Gamble*; John Gray, *False Dawn: The Delusions of Global Capitalism* (New York: The New Press, 1998); David Stockman, *The Triumph of Politics: How the Reagan Revolution Failed* (New York: Harper & Row, 1986); and Allen Schick, "Bush's Budget Problem" (paper prepared for Conference on the George W. Bush Presidency, Princeton University, April 25, 2003), www.wws.princeton.edu/bush conf/SchickPaper.pdf (accessed October 18, 2007). On the origins of neoliberalism, see David Harvey, "Neoliberalism as Creative Destruc-tion," *The Annals of the American Academy of Political and Social Science* 610, 1 (2007): 21–44; and Harvey, *Short History of Neoliberalism*. On

immigration, see Ruben G. Rumbaut, "Origins and Destinies: Immigration to the United States Since World War II," *Sociological Forum* 9, 4 (1994): 583–621.

18. Vincent Ferraro and Melissa Rosser, "Global Debt and Third World Development," in *World Security: Challenges for a New Century,* ed. Michael Klare and Daniel Thomas, 332–355 (New York: St. Martin's Press, 1994). The high point of oil prices—around $30/barrel in 1980 ($104 in 2008 dollars)—was only recently breached in March 2008, as oil futures reached new highs, stimulated by speculation and the decline in the value of the U.S. dollar.

19. On flexible production, see Michael J. Piore and Charles F. Sabel, *The Second Industrial Divide: Possibilities for Prosperity* (New York: Basic, 1986). On the Japanese "challenge," see Paul M. Kennedy, *The Rise and Fall of the Great Powers: Economic Change and Military Conflict from 1500 to 2000* (New York: Random House, 1987). The implications of global "dollarization" are addressed in chapter 6.

20. Hudson, *Super Imperialism*, esp. introduction and ch. 13. Charles Maier (*Among Empires*) suggests that the American willingness to absorb the surplus goods of other producers amounts to a "public good." It is the cost to Asia and Europe of keeping the global economy buoyant.

21. On the end of the USSR, see Walter C. Uhler, "A Review of: Once Again: How the Cold War Ended and Why the Soviet Union Collapsed," *The Journal of Slavic Military Studies* 18, 3 (2005): 505–524. On the costs and risks of the nuclear arsenal, see Stephen Schwartz, ed., *Atomic Audit—The Costs and Consequences of U.S. Nuclear Weapons Since 1940* (Washington, D.C.: Brookings Institution Press, 1998). In *The Peace of Illusions*, Christopher Layne argues that U.S. strategy in Europe would not have differed very much even had there been no Soviet "threat" (p. 71). On China, see G. John Ikenberry, "The Rise of China and the Future of the West," *Foreign Affairs* 87, 1 (January/February 2008): 23–37.

22. David S. Sorensen, *Shutting Down the Cold War: The Politics of Military Base Closure* (London: Palgrave Macmillan, 1998), 182.

23. Gaddis, *The Cold War*; Sorensen, *Shutting Down the Cold War*; and Marshall I. Goldman, "Gorbachev the Economist," *Foreign Affairs* 69, 2 (Spring 1990): 28–44. On "Team B," see Anne Hessing Cahn, *Killing Détente: The Right Attacks the CIA* (University Park, Pa.: Penn State Press, 1998). The contradiction in efforts to foster defense conversion to civilian goods was reflected in the very expensive toilet seats and other products produced by U.S. military corporations. In the Soviet Union, there was a pent-up demand for civilian goods that mil-

itary factories might be able to supply; in the United States, plenty of washing machines and refrigerators were available from civilian sources (even if they were subsidiaries of corporations that also produced military goods, e.g., General Electric).

24. National and cross-border statistics continue to be those most assiduously collected, compiled, and analyzed; intrafirm statistics are considered proprietary and are hardly available at all. On doubts about globalization, see Paul Hirst and Grahame Thompson, *Globalization in Question,* 2nd ed. (Oxford: Blackwell, 1999); and Justin Rosenberg, *The Follies of Globalization Theory* (London: Verso, 2002). French regulation theorists would invert the argument about the U.S. Constitution in the next paragraph: the Founding Fathers sought a constitutional order that would stabilize social relations to the advantage of elites, something that the Articles of Confederation were unable to accomplish. But struggle among social forces did not disappear. On regulation theory, see Robert Boyer and Yves Saillard, eds., *Régulation Theory: The State of the Art* (London: Routledge, 2002); on social struggles, see Sandra Halperin, *War and Social Change in Modern Europe* (Cambridge, England: Cambridge University Press, 2004).

25. On economic constitutionalism, see Stephen Gill, "Globalization, Market Civilization and Disciplinary Neo-Liberalism," in *Power and Resistance in the New World Order* (Houndsmill Basingstoke, England: Palgrave Macmillan, 2003), 116–142; Kanishka Jayasuriya, "Globalisation, Sovereignty, and the Rule of Law: From Political to Economic Constitutionalism?" *Constellations* 8, 4 (2001): 442–460.

Chapter 3

1. On globalization, see Paul Hirst and Grahame Thompson, *Globalization in Question,* 2nd ed. (Oxford: Blackwell, 1999); and Joseph E. Stiglitz, *Globalization and Its Discontents* (New York: Norton, 2002). Sometimes governments stop collecting statistics, as the U.S. government has done with respect to certain aspects of the money supply; see Federal Reserve Board H.6 Money Stock Measures, "Discontinuance of M3," Federal Reserve Statistical Release, November 10, 2005, revised March 9, 2006, www.federalreserve.gov/Releases/h6/discm3.htm (accessed December 13, 2006). On flows and change: It is the *change* in the means of production and social relations of capitalist societies that alters the magnitude of flows of *factors* of production and consumption. Such flows are *dependent* variables, and not causal. On

status and churn, see J. M. Balkin, "The Constitution of Status," *The Yale Law Journal* 106, 8 (June 1997): 2313–2274; Joseph Schumpeter, *Capitalism, Socialism and Democracy* (New York: Harper, 1942); Katherine Boo, "The Churn: Creative Destruction in a Border Town," *The New Yorker*, March 29, 2004, 62–73; "The Best Job in Town: The Americanization of Chennai," *The New Yorker*, July 5, 2004, 54–69; and W. Michael Cox and Richard Alm, "The Churn—The Paradox of Progress," Federal Reserve Bank of Dallas, Reprint from *1992 Annual Report*, www.dallasfed.org/fed/annual/1999p/ar92.pdf (accessed December 6, 2005). An ancillary but extremely important effect of this process is the emergence of social movements; see Ronnie D. Lipschutz, with James K. Rowe, *Globalization, Governmentality and Global Politics—Regulation for the Rest of Us?* (London: Routledge, 2005). A wonderful novelized account of globalization appears in Neal Stephenson's *Baroque Trilogy*, which tracks the expansion of English capitalism throughout the world in the late seventeenth and early eighteenth centuries. Big books, hard reading, highly recommended!

2. Karl Marx and Friedrich Engels, *The Communist Manifesto* (New York: Pocket Books, 1848/1964); and Karl Marx and Friedrich Engels, *The German Ideology,* ed. C. J. Arthur (New York: International Publishers, 1932/1970). The British have a marvelous word for losing one's job: to be made "redundant." See Neasa MacErlean and Lisa Bachelor, "Lost Your Job? Here's How to Get Back on the Road to Work," *The Observer*, April 24, 2005, http://money.guardian.co.uk/work/howto/story/0,1469825,00.html (accessed October 22, 2007). Thomas Frank, *What's the Matter with Kansas? How Conservatives Won the Heart of America* (New York: Metropolitan Books, 2004).

3. On class analysis and class in America, see Adam David Morton, "The Grimly Comic Riddle of Hegemony in IPE: Where Is Class Struggle?" *Politics* 26, 1 (2006): 62–72, and the subsequent exchange between Randall Germain and Morton in the same journal; and Janny Scott and David Leonhardt, "Class in America: Shadowy Lines that Still Divide," *New York Times*, May 15, 2005, www.nytimes.com /2005/05/15/national/class/OVERVIEWFINAL.html?ex=11352276 00&en=bf8e0a8c461091e8&ei=5070 (accessed May 16, 2005). On social forces and struggle, see Ronnie D. Lipschutz, "Capitalism, Conflict and Churn: How the American Culture War Went Global," in *World Cultures Yearbook 2007: Cultures, Conflict and Globalization,* ed. H. Anheier and Y. R. Isar, 185–196 (London: Sage, 2007); and Lipschutz, *Globalization, Governmentality and Global Politics.*

4. Stephen Gill, "Globalization, Market Civilization and Disciplinary Neo-Liberalism," in *Power and Resistance in the New World Order*

(Houndsmill, Basingstoke, UK: Palgrave Macmillan, 2003), 116–142; and Kanishka Jayasuriya, "Globalisation, Sovereignty, and the Rule of Law: From Political to Economic Constitutionalism?" *Constellations* 8, 4 (2001): 442–460. Andrew Bacevich argues that strategic policy did not drift during the 1990s; see *American Empire—The Realities and Consequences of U.S. Diplomacy* (Cambridge, Mass.: Harvard University Press, 2002).

5. Stephen K. Vogel, *Freer Markets, More Rules: Regulatory Reform in Advanced Industrial Countries* (Ithaca, N.Y.: Cornell University Press, 1996); The "Global Compact" (www.unglobalcompact.org/) was the brainchild of John G. Ruggie, a multilateralist if ever there was one; see John G. Ruggie, "The Theory and Practice of Learning Networks: Corporate Social Responsibility and the Global Compact," *Journal of Corporate Citizenship* 5 (2002): 27–36, http://greenleafpublishing.com/content/pdfs/jcc05rugg.pdf (accessed November 11, 2007); and Michael Likosky and Michael Shtender-Auerbach, "When American Corporations Deliver U.S. Foreign Policy . . . . ," *San Francisco Chronicle*, November 2, 2007, www.sfgate.com/cgi-bin/article.cgi?file=/c/a/2007/11/02/EDQGT3KJL.DTL (accessed November 11, 2007).

6. On the global republic, see Ronnie D. Lipschutz, "The Clash of Governmentalities: The Fall of the UN Republic and America's Reach for Imperium," *Contemporary Security Policy* 23, 2 (December 2002): 214–231. On the transformation of state sovereignty, see, e.g., Susan Strange, *The Retreat of the State: The Diffusion of Power in the World Economy* (Cambridge, England: Cambridge University Press, 1996). The literature on global governance is vast; the seminal book on the subject is probably James N. Rosenau and Ernst-Otto Czempiel, eds., *Governance without Government: Order and Change in World Politics* (Cambridge, England: Cambridge University Press, 1992).

7. To put the point more clearly, *political economy* is about defining the structure of the game, as opposed to the rules by which points are accumulated; see below and Lipschutz, *Globalization, Governmentality and Global Politics,* esp. chs. 2 and 3. Smith mentioned the Invisible Hand only once in *The Wealth of Nations,* yet it is that appendage for which he is best remembered; see Emma Rothschild's discussion "The Bloody and Invisible Hand," in *Economic Sentiments: Adam Smith, Condorcet, and the Enlightenment* (Cambridge, Mass.: Harvard University Press, 2001), ch. 5, 115–156, www.compilerpress.atfreeweb.com/Anno%20Rothschild%20Bloody%20&%20Invisible%201.htm (accessed November 2, 2007). Another Neal Stephenson novel, *Snow Crash* (1992), offers an imaginative vision of a hypercapitalist, self-regulating world without rule and ultimately threatened by that lack.

8. Much of this and subsequent paragraphs are based on Michel Foucault's work on discipline and governmentality, and those implications I draw for global politics and political economy. See Michel Foucault, "Governmentality," in *The Essential Foucault,* ed. Paul Rabinow and Nikolas Rose, 229–245 (New York: The New Press, 2003); Mitchell Dean, *Governmentality: Power and Rule in Modern Society* (London: Sage, 1999); and Bob Jessop, "From Micro-Powers to Governmentality: Foucault's Work on Statehood, State Formation, Statecraft and State Power," *Political Geography* 26 (2007): 34–40. Note that self-discipline is not the same as Polanyi's critique of the fantasy of "self-regulating" markets, which, in their idealized form, are homeostatic mechanisms based on flows of gold among countries and have little to do with individual behavior.

9. George W. Bush, "President Announces Tough New Enforcement Initiatives for Reform," July 9, 2002, www.whitehouse.gov/news /releases/2002/07/print/20020709-4.html (accessed April 22, 2004).

10. To invoke Stephen Krasner in a somewhat different context, "International regimes are defined as principles, norms, rules, and decision-making procedures around which actor expectations converge in a given issue-area." "Structural Causes and Regime Consequences: Regimes as Intervening Variables," in *International Regimes,* ed. Stephen D. Krasner, 1–21 (Ithaca, N.Y.: Cornell University Press, 1983), p. 1.

11. "They're f—g taking all the money back from you guys?" complains an Enron employee on the tapes. "All the money you guys stole from those poor grandmothers in California?" "Yeah, grandma Millie, man." "Yeah, now she wants her f—g money back for all the power you've charged right up, jammed right up her a— for f—g $250 a megawatt hour," www.cbsnews.com/stories/2004/06/01/evening news/main620626.shtml (accessed November 10, 2007; deletions in original). Moreover, such behavior is hardly limited to the market as it is commonly understood; the actions and activities of private security contractors in both New Orleans and Iraq also demonstrate a near-total lack of social self-discipline.

12. On commodification of the body, see Lesley A. Sharp, "The Commodification of the Body and Its Parts," *Annual Review of Anthropology* 29 (2000): 287–328. On conservative views of human nature and the market, see Jerry Z. Muller, *The Mind and the Market: Capitalism in Western Thought* (New York: Knopf, 2002). On some of the early debates about virtue and the market, see J. G. A. Pocock, *Virtue, Commerce, and History: Essays on Political Thought and History* (Cambridge, Mass.: Cambridge University Press, 1985), chs. 3, 6.

13. Adam Smith, *The Theory of Moral Sentiments* (1759), Pt. III, Sec. 1, § 111–112, www.econlib.org/Library/Smith/smMS.html (accessed November 2, 2007).

14. Joe Creech, *Righteous Indignation: Religion and the Populist Revolution* (Urbana: University of Illinois Press, 2006); Peter H. Argersinger, *The Limits of Agrarian Radicalism: Western Populism and American Politics* (Lawrence: University Press of Kansas, 1995); Martin J. Sklar, *The Corporate Reconstruction of American Capitalism 1890–1916: The Market, the Law and Politics* (Cambridge, England: Cambridge University Press, 1988); and Emily S. Rosenberg, *Spreading the American Dream: American Economic and Cultural Expansion, 1890–1945* (New York: Hill and Wang, 1982).

15. The reluctance to cooperate was most apparent in the agreements pressed by the United States on allies and clients regarding jurisdiction of the new International Criminal Court over American troops and officials. As was written in the 2002 *National Security Strategy*: "We will take the actions necessary to ensure that our efforts to meet our global security commitments and protect Americans are not impaired by the potential for investigations, inquiry, or prosecution by the International Criminal Court (ICC), whose jurisdiction does not extend to Americans and which we do not accept. We will work together with other nations to avoid complications in our military operations and cooperation, through such mechanisms as multilateral and bilateral agreements that will protect U.S. nationals from the ICC. We will implement fully the American Servicemembers Protection Act, whose provisions are intended to ensure and enhance the protection of U.S. personnel and officials [§9.5]." See The White House, *The National Security Strategy of the United States,* September 2002, p. 31, www.white house.gov/nsc/nss.pdf (accessed September 30, 2002). On the influence of Strauss, see Anne Norton, *Leo Strauss and the Politics of American Empire* (New Haven, Conn.: Yale University Press, 2004). PNAC can be found at www.newamericancentury.org/ (accessed November 5, 2007). On the syncretism of ideology and interests, see Anatole Lieven, *America Right or Wrong—An Anatomy of American Nationalism* (Oxford: Oxford University Press, 2004).

16. On vulnerability and disruption, see Ronnie D. Lipschutz, "Terror in the Suites—Narratives of Fear and the Political Economy of Danger," *Global Society* 13, 4 (October 1999): 411–439. On "risk society," see the work of Ulrich Beck, especially his seminal *Risk Society: Towards a New Modernity*, trans. Mark Ritter (London: Sage, 2002).

17. On the self-discipline problem, see Ronnie D. Lipschutz, *After Authority—War, Peace and Global Politics in the 21st Century* (Albany:

State University of New York Press, 2000), 133–154; on terrorists' use of the tools of global capitalism, see The 9/11 Commission, *Final Report of the National Commission on Terrorist Attacks upon the United States* (New York: Norton, 2004). A favored trope was "catastrophic terrorism," as expressed in Anthony Lake's *Six Nightmares: Real Threats in a Dangerous World and How America Can Meet Them* (Boston: Little, Brown, 2000). On "redefining security," see Ronnie D. Lipschutz, ed., *On Security* (New York: Columbia University Press, 1995). Bacevich is especially critical of efforts to "redefine security" during the 1990s; see *American Empire.*

18. The "electronic Pearl Harbor" was one often-suggested scenario, in which a host of well-coordinated hackers could bring down the world's computer systems; for an example, see the film *Live Free or Die Hard*, in which a disgruntled security consultant manages to crash all of America's electronic net. A fully surveilled, self-protecting system would probably have to impose strict limits on producers, consumers, and markets; the impacts of such regulation were seen in the three-day grounding of airplanes over the United States following the 9/11 attacks. On blaming agents for structural vulnerabilities, see Johann Galtung, *Human Rights in Another Key* (Cambridge, England: Polity, 1995), ch. 2; on pursuit of evil individuals and organizations, see Daniel Pipes, "Why the Japanese Internment Still Matters," *New York Sun*, December 28, 2004, www.danielpipes.org/article/2309 (accessed November 5, 2007); on ignoring the role of counterterrorist violence in creating new cadres of antisystemic agents, see Bryan Bender, "Study Cites Seeds of Terror in Iraq—War Radicalized Most, Probes Find," *The Boston Globe*, July 17, 2005, www.boston.com/news/world/articles/2005/07/17/study_cites_seeds_of_terror_in_iraq/ (accessed July 18, 2005). For a discussion of recent rethinking of force and counterterterrorism, see Eric Schmitt and Thom Shanker, "U.S. Adapts Cold-War Idea to Fight Terrorists," *New York Times*, March 18, 2008, www.nytimes.com/2008/03/18/washington/18terror.html? (accessed March 19, 2008).

19. On identity and status, see Balkin, "The Constitution of Status." On property and selfhood, see John Locke, *Two Treatises of Government,* ed. Peter Laslett (Cambridge, England: Cambridge University Press, 1988); G. W. F. Hegel, *Philosophy of Right,* trans. S.-W. Dyde (Kitchener, Ont.: Batoche Books, 2001), http://socserv.mcmaster.ca/econ/ugcm/3ll3/hegel/right.pdf (accessed November 5, 2007); C. B. Macpherson, *The Political Theory of Possessive Individualism: Hobbes to Locke* (Oxford: Oxford University Press, 1962); and Pocock, *Virtue,*

Commerce, and History. On social movements, see Lipschutz, *Globalization, Governmentality and Global Politics.*

20. It might be more accurate to call 9/11 a "failure of imagination," inasmuch as the possibility of plane bombs had been broached in other places but never taken fully seriously. The Bush administration's definition of "intelligence," according to Bob Woodward, is an interesting one: not "facts" but "judgments." Referring to Stu Cohen, acting chairman of the National Intelligence Council in 2002, Bob Woodward wrote that, "Ironclad evidence in the intelligence business is scarce and analysts need to be able to make judgments beyond the ironclad." See *Plan of Attack* (New York: Simon & Schuster, 2004), 197.

21. The key here is the realist distinction between capability and intent. It is much easier to determine the former than to divine the latter. On the acquisition of terrorist capabilities, see Richard A. Falkenrath, Robert D. Newman, and Bradley A. Thayer, *America's Achilles' Heel—Nuclear, Biological, and Chemical Terrorism and Covert Attack* (Cambridge, Mass.: MIT Press, 1998): 171–172, 173; Ronnie D. Lipschutz and Heather Turcotte, "Duct Tape or Plastic? The Political Economy of Threats and the Production of Fear," in *Making Threats—Biofears and Environmental Anxieties,* ed. Betsy Harmann, Banu Subramaniam, and Charles Zerner, 25–46 (Lanham, Md.: Rowman & Littlefield, 2005); and Ronnie D. Lipschutz, "Imperial Warfare in the Naked City— Sociality Organizations and Networks as Critical Infrastructures," *International Political Sociology* (forthcoming, 2008). Finally, consider the story of Hamid Hayat of Lodi, California, sentenced to twenty-four years in prison because, according to the prosecution, he had "a jihadi heart." John Diaz, "The Phantom Terrorist Camp," *San Francisco Chronicle,* September 16, 2007, www.sfgate.com/cgibin/article.cgi?file= /c/a/2007/09/16/ED85S5JL3.DTL (accessed September 20, 2007).

22. On the transformation of security, see Lipschutz, *After Authority* and *On Security.* On the potential use of WMDs in cities, see Falkenrath, Newman, and Thayer, *America's Achilles' Heel;* and Graham Allison, *Nuclear Terrorism: The Ultimate Preventable Catastrophe* (New York: Times Books, 2004).

23. On economic citizenship, see Stephen Gill, "The Global Panopticon? The Neoliberal State, Economic Life, and Democratic Surveillance," *Alternatives* 2, 1 (January–March 1995): 1–50.

24. Friedrich List, *National System of Political Economy,* trans. G. A. Matile (Philadelphia: J.B. Lippincott, 1856). An example of the supposed power of the individual can be seen in the film *Live Free or Die Hard.*

Chapter 4

1. The 9/11 Commission, *Final Report of the National Commission on Terrorist Attacks upon the United States* (New York: Norton, 2004). In early 2008 this problem had arisen with respect to the government of Pakistani President Musharraf and the Bush administration's efforts to urge or force him to "democratize," which led to entirely unexpected results and, perhaps, Musharraf's exit from office. Nonetheless, by what right—aside from the $10 billion provided to Pakistan—does the United States seek to impose its will on a notionally sovereign state? The locution "unknown unknowns" is former U.S. Secretary of Defense Donald Rumsfeld's: "There are no knowns. There are things we know that we know. There are known unknowns—that is to say, there are things that we now know we don't know but there are also unknown unknowns. There are things we do not know we don't know. So when we do the best we can and we pull all this information together, and we then say well that's basically what we see as the situation, that is really only the known knowns and the known unknowns. And each year we discover a few more of those unknown unknowns." "Rumsfeld Baffles Press with 'Unknown Unknowns,'" *ABC News Online* (Australian Broadcasting Corp.), June 7, 2003, www.abc.net. au/news/newsitems/s576186.htm (accessed August 28, 2003).

2. Historically, the international "right of hot pursuit" has applied only to ships that have violated territorial waters but have fled to the high seas; application of this principle across national borders has been invoked by some analysts, but in the words of Peter Danchin at the University of Maryland School of Law, "This idea of 'hot pursuit' is just an attempt to twist the law of the sea doctrine into a self-defense idea." Cited in Lionel Beehner, "Can States Invoke 'Hot Pursuit' to Hunt Rebels?" Council on Foreign Relations Backgrounder, June 7, 2007, www.cfr.org/publication/13440/ (accessed November 15, 2007). See also Anne Orford, "The Destiny of International Law," *Leiden Journal of International Law* 17 (2004): 441–476; Jean L. Cohen, "Whose Sovereignty? Empire versus International Law," *Ethics and International Affairs* 18, 3 (2004): 1–24.

3. Of especial interest is the question of whether this principle applies to U.S. citizens within the sovereign jurisdiction of the United States. In *Hamdi v. Rumsfeld,* the U.S. Supreme Court concluded that it did. But Hamdi was released and repatriated to Saudi Arabia on condition that he give up his U.S. citizenship. See Supreme Court of the United States, *Hamdi et al. v. Rumsfeld, Secretary of Defense, et al.,* No. 03-6696. Argued April 28, 2004—decided June 28, 2004, www.supreme

courtus.gov/opinions/03pdf/03-6696.pdf (accessed November 14, 2007). In the case of José Padilla, the government moved the defendant from civil to military imprisonment to avoid such legal difficulties; in January 2008 he was tried, convicted, and sentenced in federal court to seventeen years in prison. See David Cole, "Double Standards, Democracy, and Human Rights," *Peace Review* 18, 4 (2006): 427–437.

4. "Global governance" is a term, popular during the 1990s but in decline since 2001, that invoked something more along the lines of multilateral regulation and management of the world's affairs, in which the United States was *primus inter pares*. See the special issue "Global Governance and Public Accountability," *Government and Opposition* 39, 2 (2004), www.blackwell-synergy.com/toc/goop/39/2 (accessed December 17, 2007); James N. Rosenau and Ernst-Otto Czempiel, eds., *Governance without Government: Order and Change in World Politics* (Cambridge, England: Cambridge University Press, 1992); and Martin Hewson and Timothy J. Sinclair, eds., *Approaches to Global Governance Theory* (Albany: State University of New York Press, 1999).

5. George W. Bush, "Address to a Joint Session of Congress and the American People," www.whitehouse.gov/news/releases/2001/09/200 10920-8.html (accessed July 2, 2006).

6. In this respect, the GWOT is much like the "war" on cancer and the "war" on drugs, designed to provide the illusion of action in the face of intense demands for results. The State Department's efforts to capture the hearts and minds of Muslims through public diplomacy under the aegis of presidential friends such as Karen Hughes and others illustrates the public relations quality of the GWOT. See, e.g., Linda Feldman, "Can Karen Hughes Help U.S. Image Abroad?" *Christian Science Monitor*, March 16, 2005, www.csmonitor.com/2005/0316/ p03s01-usfp.html (accessed December 10, 2007); and Fred Kaplan, "Heck of a Job, Hughsie—Karen Hughes Throws in the Towel," *Slate*, November 1, 2007, www.slate.com/id/2177248/ (accessed December 10, 2007). On the capabilities of the Special Forces, see the U.S. Special Operations Command Web site, www.socom.mil/ (accessed December 20, 2007). On secrets, see Joseph Weisberg, "CIA's Open Secrets," *New York Times*, August 27, 2007, www.nytimes.com/ 2007/08/27/opinion/27weisberg.html (accessed August 29, 2007).

7. On the metastasis of terrorism, see the New York Police Department Intelligence Division's interesting study of "homegrown terrorism" by Mitchell D. Silver and Arvin Bhatt, "Radicalization in the West—The Homegrown Threat," 2007, www.nypdshield.org/public /SiteFiles/documents/NYPD_ReportRadicalization_in_the_West.pdf (accessed December 12, 2007). See also Eric Geiger, "Germany Sees

Alarming Threat from Citizens Who Convert to Islam," *San Francisco Chronicle*, September 7, 2007, www.sfgate.com/cgi-bin/article .cgi?file=/c/a/2007/09/07/MN0LRP6S4.DTL (accessed September 7, 2007); Monstersandcritics.com, "Germans Watch Rising Conversion to Islam with Concern," September 6, 2007, http://news.monstersand critics.com/europe/news/article_1352428.php/SIDEBAR_Germans_ watch_rising_conversion_to_Islam_with_concern (accessed September 15, 2007); and Regina Kerner, "Unter Beobachtung Nach den Festnahmen im Sauerland wird die Frage debattiert, ob zum Islam übergetretene Deutsche besonders anfällig sind für Radikalismus," *Berliner Zeitung,* September 6, 2007, www.berlinonline.de/berliner-zei tung/print/tagesthema/683848.html (accessed September 15, 2007).

8. I discuss the notion of networks of knowledge and practice, and epistemes, in several of my books and articles, especially (with Judith Mayer), *Global Civil Society and Global Environmental Governance* (Albany: State University of New York Press, 1996). See also chapter 5.

9. On Pakistan, see, e.g., K. Alan Kronstadt and Bruce Vaugh, "Terrorism in South Asia," Congressional Research Service RL32259, December 13, 2004, http://stinet.dtic.mil/cgibin/GetTRDoc?AD= ADA444777&Location=U2&doc=GetTRDoc.pdf (ac-cessed December 12, 2007); and Nicholas Schmidle, "Next-Gen Taliban," *New York Times Magazine,* January 6, 2008, www.nytimes.com/2008/01/06/mag azine/06PAKISTAN-t.html? (ac (accessed January 5, 2008). On rendition and "black sites," see Jane Mayer, "The Black Sites," *New Yorker*, August 13, 2007, www.newyorker.com/report ing/2007/08/13/0708 13fa_fact_mayer (accessed September 26, 2007); and Leila Nadya Sadat, "Ghost Prisoners and Black Sites: Extraordinary Rendition under International Law," *Case Western Journal of International Law* 39 (2005): 309–342, www.case.edu/orgs/jil/archives/vol37no2and3/Sadat.pdf (accessed December 12, 2007). On possible charges of war crimes, see Frank Rich, "The 'Good Germans' Among Us," *New York Times*, October 14, 2007, www.nytimes.com/2007/10/14/opinion/14rich2.html (accessed October 14, 2007).

10. One admittedly leftist, and somewhat dated, account of U.S. interventions can be found in Darrel Garwood, *Under Cover: Thirty-Five Years of CIA Deception* (New York: Grove Press, 1985). William Appleman Williams, *Empire as a Way of Life* (New York: Oxford University Press, 1980) provides lists of earlier U.S. interventions, especially in the Western Hemisphere. A more recent survey is John Perkins, *The Secret History of the American Empire: Economic Hit Men, Jackals and the Truth about Global Corruption* (New York: Dutton, 2007). On continuity and change in U.S. foreign policy, see Charles S. Maier, *Among Empires—*

American Ascendancy and Its Predecessors (Cambridge, Mass.: Harvard University Press, 2006); and Andrew Bacevich, *American Empire—The Realities and Consequences of U.S. Diplomacy* (Cambridge, Mass.: Harvard University Press, 2002).

11. Thus, the United States can assert unilateral rights in disregard of domestic and international criticism and opposition. When, however, the Russian Federation tries to do the same, it is severely criticized by the United States. On the United States and international institutions, see, e.g., Rosemary Foot, S. Neil MacFarlane, and Michael Mastanduno, eds., *US Hegemony and International Organizations: The United States and Multilateral Institutions* (Oxford: Oxford University Press, 2003). I also address the issue of multilateral "cooperation" in Ronnie D. Lipschutz, *Global Environmental Politics: Power, Perspectives, and Practice* (Washington, D.C.: CQ Press, 2003).

12. See, e.g., Kevin Ruane, *The Rise and Fall of the European Defence Community: Anglo-American Relations and the Crisis of European Defence, 1950–55* (New York: St. Martin's Press, 2000); and H. W. Brands, *The Specter of Neutralism: The United States and the Emergence of the Third World, 1947–1960* (New York: Columbia University Press, 1989). Bacevich addresses isolationism in *American Empire.*

13. On isolationism and the Open Door, see William Appleman Williams, *The Tragedy of American Diplomacy,* 2nd, rev., enl. ed. (New York: Dell, 1972); and Williams, *Empire as a Way of Life.* The Atlantic Charter: "Fourth, they will endeavor, with due respect for their existing obligations, to further the enjoyment by all States, great or small, victor or vanquished, of access, on equal terms, to the trade and to the raw materials of the world which are needed for their economic prosperity," www.yale.edu/lawweb/avalon/wwii/atlantic.htm (accessed December 20, 2007). Michael Hudson, *Super Imperialism—The Origin and Fundamentals of U.S. World Dominance,* 2nd ed. (London: Pluto Press, 2003).

14. On the preference for empire, see Deepak Lal, *In Defense of Empires* (Washington, D.C.: AEI Press, 2004), www.aei.org/docLib /20040902_book790text.pdf (accessed July 10, 2005); and Niall Ferguson, *Colossus—The Rise and Fall of the American Empire* (New York: Penguin, 2005). On U.S. subsidies to the French war in Indochina, see, e.g., G. V. C. Naidu, "Vietnam: Ten Years after Victory," *Social Scientist* 13, 5 (May 1985): 59.

15. On the autonomy problem, see Robert H. Jackson, *Quasi-states, Sovereignty, International Relations and the Third World* (Cambridge, England: Cambridge University Press, 1990); and Ricardo Soares de Oliveira, *Oil and Politics in the Gulf of Guinea* (New York: Columbia University Press, 2007). On the problem of interpreting academic the-

ories for policy makers, see Alexander George, *Bridging the Gap—Theory and Practice in Foreign Policy* (Washington, D.C.: U.S. Institution of Peace Press, 1993). On the suitability of highly educated individuals for public policy positions, see David C. Engerman, "Bernath Lecture: American Knowledge and Global Power," *Diplomatic History* 31, 4 (2007): 599–622.

16. On the supposed virtues of development theory and practice, see Robert A. Packenham, *Liberal America and the Third World: Political Development Ideas in Foreign Aid and Social Science* (Princeton, N.J.: Princeton University Press, 1973).

17. Apparently, Kissinger said this in a National Security Council meeting on June 27, 1970. Although the statement can be found all over the Internet, a specific source cannot. Nowadays, the blame for Africa's parlous state is laid on abysmal leadership and institutional failures, both of which involve government manipulation of the economy. For recent, and contrary, evidence that blame might be somewhat misplaced, see Celia W. Dugger, "Ending Famine, Simply by Ignoring the Experts," *New York Times*, December 2, 2007, www.nytimes.com /2007/12/02/world/africa/02malawi.html (accessed December 2, 2007).

18. As Bacevich points out, the tradition of having "Gurkhas" fight for the empire is a long one; see *American Empire.*

19. One can view these groupings as offering trade-offs: changes in some aspects of sovereignty in exchange for greater sovereignty in others. Although it is conventional wisdom that everyone is better off as a result, to my knowledge, no one has actually tried to do a detailed accounting of the costs and benefits of such trade-offs.

20. Perhaps this somewhat fictionalized notion of "sovereign states in anarchy" was a way of eliding the extent to which many countries already lacked much in the way of classical sovereignty.

21. On Congo, for example, see Stephen R. Weissman, *American Foreign Policy in the Congo, 1960–1964* (Ithaca, N.Y.: Cornell University Press, 1974).

22. The classical texts of functionalism are Ernst B. Haas, *Beyond the Nation-State: Functionalism and International Organization* (Stanford, Calif.: Stanford University Press, 1964); and David Mitrany, *A Working Peace System* (Chicago: Quadrangle, 1966).

23. On the neoconservative view of Europe, see Robert Kagan, *Of Paradise and Power—America and Europe in the New World Order* (New York: Knopf, 2003).

24. Bruce D. Larkin, personal communication, May 15, 1997; see also Ronnie D. Lipschutz, "(B)orders and (Dis)orders: The Role of

Moral Authority in Global Politics," in *Identities, Borders, Orders—Rethinking International Relations Theory,* ed. Mathias Albert, David Jacobson and Yosef Lapid, 73–90 (Minneapolis: University of Minnesota Press, 2001). Again, Bacevich offers considerable insight into the role of gunboat diplomacy and intervention in today's Imperium; see *American Empire,* especially chapters 5 and 6.

25. On border security, see Scott Shane, "Canadian Border Proves Difficult to Secure," *New York Times,* June 5, 2006, www.nytimes.com/2006/06/05/world/americas/05border.html (accessed December 12, 2007); and David McLemore, "Tales of Terrorists Breaching Border Overblown, So Far," *Dallas Morning News,* December 11, 2007, www.dallasnews.com/sharedcontent/dws/dn/latestnews/stories/121007dnintborderterror.2c2f8e7.html (accessed December 12, 2007).

26. On identifying terrorists before they act, see, e.g., Robert Popp et al., "Countering Terrorism through Information Technology," *Communications of the ACM* 47, 3 (March 2004): 35–43, http://delivery.acm.org/10.1145/980000/971642/p36popp.pdf?key1=971642&key=1198057911&coll=GUIDE&dl=GUIDE&CFID=46637589&CFTOKEN=12923375 (accessed December 12, 2007). On terrorist trials in the United States, see "Terrorist Trials: A Report Card," Center on Law and Security, NYU Law School, February 2005, www.lawandsecurity.org/publications/terroristtrialreportcard.pdf (accessed December 12, 2007); and Karen J. Greenberg with Daniel Freifeld, "Terrorist Trials, 2001–2007: Lessons Learned," Center on Law and Security, NYU Law School, October 2007, www.lawandsecurity.org/publications/TTRC2007Update1.pdf (accessed December 12, 2007). More recently, German and British authorities have begun to disrupt supposed plots in the planning stages.

27. The Clinton administration signed the Rome Treaty, but the Bush administration, in effect, "unsigned" the treaty. See John R. Bolton, "The United States and the International Criminal Court" (remarks to the Federalist Society, Washington, D.C., November 14, 2002), www.state.gov/t/us/rm/15158.htm (accessed November 30, 2007); and Edward T. Swaine, "Unsigning," *Stanford Law Review* 55, 5 (2003): 2061–2090. On classified evidence, see, e.g., Norman Abrams, "The Military Commissions Saga," *Journal of International Criminal Justice* 5, 1 (2007): 2–9. This is a special issue of the journal that addresses prosecution of terrorists by the United States.

28. The White House, *The National Security Strategy of the United States,* September 2002, pp. ii, iii.

Chapter 5

1. On "change," see Thomas A. Birkland, "'The World Changed Today': Agenda-Setting and Policy Change in the Wake of the September 11 Terrorist Attacks," *Review of Policy Research* 21, 2 (2004): 179–200. On Indian summer and war, see Philip Bobbitt, *The Shield of Achilles—War, Peace, and the Course of History* (New York: Knopf, 2002), 819.

2. Carl Schmitt, *Political Theology: Four Chapters on the Concept of Sovereignty* (Cambridge, Mass: MIT Press, 1965). Commentaries on and studies of Carl Schmitt and his arguments are now legion. Perhaps the best examination of Schmitt is Gopal Balakrishnan, *The Enemy: An Intellectual Portrait of Carl Schmitt* (London: Verso, 2000). See also Jef Huysmans, "International Politics of Insecurity: Normativity, Inwardness and the Exception," *Security Dialogue* 37, 1 (March 2006): 11–29; and Roland Axtmann, "Humanity or Enmity? Carl Schmitt on International Politics," *International Politics* 44, 5 (September 2007): 531–551. On who is the "decider," see Ed Henry and Barbara Starr, "Bush: 'I'm the Decider' on Rumsfeld," *CNN.com*, April 18, 2006, www.cnn.com/2006/POLITICS/04/18/rumsfeld/ (accessed July 15, 2006).

3. Compare, for example, Frederick A. O. Schwartz Jr. and Aziz Z. Huq, *Unchecked and Unbalanced—Presidential Power in a Time of Terror* (New York: The New Press, 2007); and Dinesh D'Souza, *The Enemy at Home—The Cultural Left and Its Responsibility for 9/11* (New York: Doubleday, 2007).

4. I do not refer here to the "history of terrorism," which some claim began with the Jewish Zealots and the Ismaili Hashishin; the record of nonstate actors attacking states is a long one, depending on how one conceptualizes "nonstate actors." For a brief discussion of this "history," see Ronnie D. Lipschutz and Heather Turcotte, "States of Terror: Framing Threats and Selling Fears" (presented at a panel on "Threat Politics III: Frames, Language and Context," 46th Annual Convention of the International Studies Association, Honolulu, Hawaii, March 1–5, 2005). On the definition of terrorism in international law, see, e.g., Antonio Cassese, "The Multifaceted Criminal Notion of Terrorism in International Law," *Journal of International Criminal Justice* (December 2006), http://jicj.oxfordjournals.org/cgi/reprint/mql074v1 (accessed December 14, 2007).

5. On the war in Afghanistan, see Steve Coll, *Ghost Wars: The Secret History of the CIA, Afghanistan, and Bin Laden, from the Soviet Invasion to September 10, 2001* (New York: Penguin, 2004).

6. Although Andrew Bacevich never addresses the "state of exception," he does provide a useful background of the military and social

considerations behind the declaration of the GWOT; see *The New American Militarism: How Americans Are Seduced by War* (Oxford: Oxford University Press, 2005).

7. On mobile bombs, see Mike Davis, *Buda's Wagon—A Brief History of the Car Bomb* (London: Verso, 2007).

8. The iconic film about rogue nukes is the 2002 *Sum of All Fears*, based on a novel by Tom Clancy. For examples of warnings about the threat of nuclear terrorism, see Graham Allison, *Nuclear Terrorism: The Ultimate Preventable Catastrophe* (New York: Times Books, 2004); and Michael Levi, *On Nuclear Terrorism* (Cambridge, Mass.: Harvard University Press, 2007).

9. See, e.g., Lisa Hajjer, "From Nuremberg to Guantánamo: International Law and American Power Politics," *Middle East Report* 229 (Winter, 2003): 8–15; and Uprenda Baxi, "The 'War *on* Terror' and the 'WAR *of* Terror': Nomadic Multitudes, Aggressive Incumbents, and the 'New' International Law," *Osgoode Hall Law Journal* 43, 1 and 2 (2005): 7–43. See also Joseph Wilson, *The Politics of Truth* (New York: Carroll & Graf, 2005).

10. According to John Yoo, "The President has broad constitutional power to take military action in response to the terrorist attacks on the United States on September 11, 2001. Congress has acknowledged this inherent executive power in both the War Powers Resolution and the Joint Resolution passed by Congress on September 14, 2001 . . . . The President has constitutional power not only to retaliate against any person, organization, or State suspected of involvement in terrorist attacks on the United States, but also against foreign States suspected of harboring or supporting such organizations. . . . The President may deploy military force preemptively against terrorist organizations or the States that harbor or support them, whether or not they can be linked to the specific terrorist incidents of September 11." John C. Yoo, Deputy Assistant Attorney General, "The President's Constitutional Authority to Conduct Military Operations against Terrorists and the Nations Supporting Them," Office of Legal Counsel, U.S. Department of Justice, September 25, 2001, www.usdoj.gov/olc/warpowers 925.htm (accessed December 14, 2007).

11. To be sure, there seem to be legal pretexts for legitimating an occupation, as opposed to an annexation. Although the UN Security Council refused to approve the American invasion of Iraq in 2003, in Resolution 1483 (May 22, 2003) it recognized the United States and Britain as the legitimate occupying powers in Iraq. How to square the two is not at all clear. On the changing ontology of war, see Andrew Bacevich, *American Empire—The Realities and Consequences of U.S.*

Diplomacy (Cambridge, Mass.: Harvard University Press, 2002); Bacevich, *New American Militarism*; E. R. Goldman, "New Threats, New Identities, and New Ways of War: The Sources of Change in National Security Doctrine," *Journal of Strategic Studies* 24, 2 (June 2001): 43–76; and Helen Dexter, "New War, Good War and the War on Terror: Explaining, Excusing and Creating Western Neo-interventionism," *Development and Change* 38, 6 (2007): 1055–1071.

12. Peter Gowan, *The Global Gamble—Washington's Faustian Bid for World Dominance* (London:Verso, 1999), 144–146. On the link between terrorism and the USSR, see Claire Sterling, *The Terror Network: The Secret War of International Terrorism* (New York: Holt, Rinehart & Winston, 1981). For a discussion of the relationship between terrorists and states, see Michel Wieviorka, *The Making of Terrorism,* trans. David Gordon White (Chicago: University of Chicago Press, 2004).

13. To be sure, during Lebanon's long-running civil war it was difficult to speak of a state or government. For more on Hezbollah, see, e.g., the article and books reviewed in Adam Shatz, "In Search of Hezbollah," *New York Review of Books* 51, 7 (April 29, 2004), www.nybooks.com/articles/17060 (accessed June 27, 2006).

14. The logic, of course, is that governments under punishment will suppress any terrorist networks that might exist within their territories; the reality is that states in which such groups are to be found often lack the capacity to suppress them, as seen in Afghanistan, Pakistan, Sri Lanka, and even India. On "networks of knowledge and practice," see Ronnie Lipschutz, with Judith Mayer, *Global Civil Society and Global Environmental Governance* (Albany: State University of New York Press, 1996). On the liquid bomb ring, see Nic Fleming, "How Terrorists Could Have Made a 'Liquid Bomb,'" *Telegraph.co.uk*, August 11, 2006, www.telegraph.co.uk/news/main.jhtml?xml=/news/2006/08/10/uchemical.xml (accessed September 16, 2007); on the hydrogen peroxide plot, see Mark Landler, "German Police Arrest 3 in Terrorist Plot," *New York Times*, September 6, 2007, www.nytimes.com/2007/09/06/world/europe/06germany.html (accessed September 16, 2007).

15. See David Altheide, "Consuming Terrorism," *Symbolic Interaction* 27, 3 (Summer 2004): 289–308; and Robert A. Zieger, "'Uncle Sam Wants You . . . to Go Shopping': A Consumer Society Responds to National Crisis, 1957–2001," *Canadian Review of American Studies* 34, 1 (2004): 83–103.

16. The White House, *The National Security Strategy of the United States,* September 2002, p. iv. There was a considerable amount of whining during the 1990s about "asymmetric threats" and why they were not cricket; Bacevich addresses these in *American Empire.*

17. On the cost of the GWOT, see Martin Wolk, "Cost of Iraq War Could Surpass $1 Trillion," MSNBC, March 14, 2006, www.msnbc. msn.com/id/11880954/ (accessed December 14, 2007); Amy Belasco, "The Cost of Iraq, Afghanistan, and Other Global War on Terror Operations Since 9/11," Congressional Research Service, November 9, 2007, RL33110, www.fas.org/sgp/crs/natsec/RL33110.pdf (accessed December 14, 2007); and Joseph E. Stiglitz and Linda J. Bilmes, *The Three Trillion Dollar War: The True Cost of the Iraq Conflict* (New York: W. W. Norton, 2008). Adjusted for inflation, World War II cost $5 trillion, the Korean War, $456 billion, the Vietnam War, $518 billion. See Leonard Doyle, "Trillion-dollar War: Afghanistan and Iraq Set to Cost More Than Vietnam and Korea," *The Independent*, October 24, 2007, http://news.independent.co.uk/world/americas/article3090340.ece (accessed December 14, 2007); and Zachary Cole, "Only World War II Was Costlier Than Iraq War," *The San Francisco Chronicle*, March 18, 2008, www.sfgae.com/cgi-bin/article cgi?file=ca2008/03/18/MNBV VL9GK.DTL (accessed March 20, 2008).

Chapter 6

1. See Michael Hudson, *Super Imperialism—The Origin and Fundamentals of U.S. World Dominance,* 2nd ed. (London: Pluto Press, 2003). For an economist's view of global dollarization, see Ronald I. McKinnon, "The World Dollar Standard and Globalization: New Rules for the Game?" in *Exchange Rates, Economic Integration and the International Economy,* ed. Leo Michelis and Mark Lovewell, 3–28 (Toronto: APF Press, 2004), www.arts.ryerson.ca/michelis/michelis-apf.pdf#page=19 (accessed December 20, 2007). On the euro, see Menzie Chinn and Jeffrey A. Frankel, "Will the Euro Eventually Surpass the Dollar as Leading International Reserve Currency?" in G7 *Current Account Imbalances: Sustainability and Adjustment,* ed. Richard H. Clarida, 283–336 (Chicago: University of Chicago Press, 2007); Gabriele Galati and Philip Wooldridge, *The Euro as a Reserve Currency: A Challenge to the Pre-eminence of the US Dollar?* BIS Working Papers No. 218 (Basel: Bank for International Settlements, October 2006), http://papers.ssrn .com/sol3/Delivery.cfm/SSRN_ID948148_code456443.pdf?abstratid =948148&mirid=1 (accessed December 15, 2007).

2. On defense spending, see BBC News, "US Senate Passes Iraq Funds Bill," December 14, 2007, news.bbc.co.uk/2/hi/americas/

7145488.stm (accessed December 14, 2007). Foreign exchange holdings by U.S. creditors have risen from about $1 trillion in 2000 to more than $2.5 trillion at the end of 2007 (this does not include foreign private holdings). Japan holds about $600 billion; China about $400 billion; the EU about $450 billion. See U.S. Treasury, "Major Foreign Holders of Treasury Securities," November 16, 2007, www.ustreas.gov/tic/mfh.txt (accessed December 15, 2007). On the risky nature of the contemporary global economy, see Susan Strange, *Casino Capitalism* (Oxford: Blackwell, 1986); and Marieke de Goede, *Virtue, Fortune, and Faith: A Genealogy of Finance* (Minneapolis: University of Minnesota Press, 2005).

3. As of mid-March 2008, the global economy had been stabilized through a largely unprecedented series of actions by the U.S. Federal Reserve Bank and others; however, because no one knows how large potential investment losses might become, there is good reason to think the worst is yet to come; see the various articles in *New York Times* from roughly March 10 through March 18, 2008. Paul Krugman has offered a series of fairly pessimistic views of the global economy's near-term prospects; see *Conscience of a Liberal* (New York: Norton, 2007); "After the Money's Gone," *New York Times*, December 14, 2007, www.nytimes.com/2007/12/14/opinion/14krugman.html?_r=1&ref=opinion& (accessed December 14, 2007); and "The B Word," *New York Times*, March 17, 2008, www.nytimes.com/2008/03/17/opinion/17krugman.html? (accessed March 17, 2008).

4. U.S. Treasury, "Schedules of Federal Debt – Daily, Unaudited," www.treasurydirect.gov/govt/reports/pd/feddebt/feddebt_daily.htm (accessed December 15, 2007). On inflation in China, see David Barboza, "China's Inflation Hits American Price Tags," *New York Times*, February 1, 2008, www.nytimes.com/2008/02/01/business/world business/01inflate.html? (accessed February 1, 2008). On the issue of debt default, see Robert Hunter Wade, "The Invisible Hand of the American Empire," *Ethics & International Affairs* 17, 2 (2003): 77–88.

5. According to the Congressional Research Service, the cost of the GWOT from 2001 to 2008 was approximately $800 billion, including expenditures of more than $600 billion on Iraq. The remainder is the cost of operations in Afghanistan and elsewhere, and what is called "enhanced security." Amy Belasco, "The Cost of Iraq, Afghanistan, and Other Global War on Terror Operations Since 9/11," Congressional Research Service, November 9, 2007, RL33110, Table 1, www.fas.org/sgp/crs/natsec/RL33110.pdf (accessed December 14, 2007).

6. In 1970 the United States held about $10 billion in gold, at the then current rate of $35/ounce. The first devaluation changed this to $42/ounce, which hardly made a dent in the problem. Today, with gold in the neighborhood of $1,000/ounce, those holdings are worth only about $300 billion, still a drop in the dollar bucket. On Bretton Woods and the dollar standard, see Hudson, *Super Imperialism*; Peter Gowan, *The Global Gamble—Washington's Faustian Bid for World Dominance* (London: Verso, 1999); and Wade, "The Invisible Hand." On gold, see Joanne Gowa, *Closing the Gold Window—Domestic Politics and the End of Bretton Woods* (Ithaca, N.Y.: Cornell University Press, 1983). On oil, see Franz Schurmann, *The Logic of World Power* (New York: Pantheon, 1974); and Daniel Yergin, *The Prize—The Epic Quest for Oil, Money and Power* (New York: Simon & Schuster, 1991).

7. Apparently some of America's creditors and oil producers are shifting a small quantity of their holdings and prices to the euro; see, e.g., Robert Looney, "The Iranian Oil Bourse: A Threat to Dollar Supremacy?" *Challenge* 50, 2 (March–April 2007): 86–109.

8. Outside of the world's major dollar creditors, there are virtually no countries that on the one hand are good credit risks and on the other hand can absorb hundreds of billions of dollars of borrowing and foreign investment. On the strategies of the Reagan administration, see David Stockman, *The Triumph of Politics: How the Reagan Revolution Failed* (New York: Harper & Row, 1986). Nixon, it should be noted, would never have fallen for the Laffer curve.

9. Compare this to the effective tax rates on many U.S. corporations, some of which are zero. See Robert McIntyre and T. D. Coo Nguyen, "Freeloaders—Declining Corporate Tax Payments in the Bush Years," *The Multinational Monitor* 25, 11 (November 2004), www .multinationalmonitor.org/mm2004/112004/mcintyre.html (accessed December 15, 2007); and William Baue, "Speaking from Both Sides of the Mouth: The Art and Science of Corporate Tax Avoidance," *Sustainability Investment News*, February 4, 2005, www.socialfunds.com/ news/article.cgi/article1630.html (accessed December 15, 2007). For an interesting perspective on "tax shopping," see "Zoom in on Corporate Tax," Deloitte, www.deloitte.com/dtt/leadership/0,1045,sid% 253D111773,00.html (accessed December 15, 2007). On legalized theft, see John Ralston Saul, *The Collapse of Globalism and the Reinvention of the World* (London: Atlantic Books, 2005); and David Harvey, *A Brief History of Neoliberalism* (Oxford: Oxford University Press, 2005).

10. On the "Nixon Doctrine," see Schurmann, *The Logic of World Power*.

11. On the balance of payments deficits, see U.S. Census Bureau, "U.S. Trade in Goods and Services—Balance of Payments, 1960–2006," www.census.gov/foreign-trade/statistics/historical/gands.txt (accessed August 23, 2007); Schurmann, *The Logic of World Power.* The oil companies' wish to reduce prices was partly the result of a price war with the Soviet Union, which was beginning to ship oil to Europe.

12. On the relationship among oil, military spending, and war, see Shimshon Bichler and Jonathan Nitzan, "Dominant Capital and the New Wars," *Journal of World Systems Research* 10, 2 (Summer 2004): 255–327, http://jwsr.ucr.edu/archive/vol10/number2/pdf/jwsrv10 n2-bandn.pdf (accessed December 15, 2007). By some estimates, $100/barrel of oil incorporates a $50–65/bbl "base" price and a $35–50/bbl speculative premium. See, e.g., Matthew Robinson, "Rising Speculation Fueling Big Oil Price Swings," *Reuters.uk*, December 21, 2007, http://uk.reuters.com/article/managerViews/idKNOA149 74920071221 (accessed December 23, 2007). Oil is also a hedge against a declining dollar.

13. Walter Pincus, "2007 Spying Said to Cost $50 Billion," *Washington Post*, October 20, 2007, A04, www.washingtonpost.com/wpdyn/content/article/2007/10/29/AR2007102902062.html (accessed December 15, 2007); and Veronique De Rugy, "Facts and Figures about Homeland Security Spending," American Enterprise Institute, December 14, 2006, www.aei.org/docLib/20061214_FactsandFigures.pdf (accessed December 15, 2007).

14. Andrew Bacevich, *The New American Militarism: How Americans Are Seduced by War* (Oxford: Oxford University Press, 2005); for the prelude to the invasion of Iraq, see Bob Woodward, *Plan of Attack* (New York: Simon & Schuster, 2004).

15. Bacevich, *New American Militarism.*

16. BBC News, "US Senate Passes Iraq Funds Bill." See also Ismael Hossein-Zadeh, "Escalating Military Spending," *Counterpunch*, April 16, 2007, www.counterpunch.org/hossein04162007.html (accessed December 15, 2007).

17. All of this ignores the fact that the military buildup is largely structured for interstate conflict—read here, with China—and plays a very small role in the GWOT. See, e.g., Robert D. Kaplan, "How We Would Fight China," *Atlantic Monthly*, June 2005, www.theatlantic .com/doc/200506/kaplan (accessed December 20, 2007).

Chapter 7

1. I do not deny that former empires used law for purposes of self-legitimation and imperial regulation; what they did not do is transform normative universalism into a globalized *legal* form. On the legitimacy of empire, see Jean Cohen, "Whose Sovereignty? Empire versus International Law," *Ethics and International Affairs* 18, 3 (2004): 1–24; Amy Kaplan, "Where Is Guantánamo?" *American Quarterly* 57, 3 (2005): 831–858; and George Steinmetz, "Return to Empire: The New U.S. Imperialism in Comparative Historical Perspective," *Sociological Theory* 23, 4 (December 2005): 339–367. Extradition of a person accused of a crime is the conventional way in which the jurisdictional issue is addressed, and there is considerable international law addressing terrorism; see Gilbert Guillame, "Terrorism and International Law," *International and Comparative Law Quarterly* 53, 3 (2004): 537–548. Recall John Yoo's statement, "What the administration is trying to do is create a new legal regime," cited in Warren Richey, "How Long Can Guantanamo Prisoners Be Held?" *Christian Science Monitor*, April 9, 2002, www.csmonitor.com/2002/0409/p01s03-usju.html (accessed March 24, 2008).

2. As noted previously, the idea that the Northwest provinces of Pakistan are "lawless" or "ungoverned" is not correct; many of its laws are local and, to some indeterminate degree, not legislated by the national government. For a protest against such kidnappings, see Hannah Arendt, *Eichmann in Jerusalem: A Report on the Banality of Evil* (New York: Viking, 1963). The risk of allowing domestic justice to work is discussed in John C. Yoo, Deputy Assistant Attorney General, "The President's Constitutional Authority to Conduct Military Operations Against Terrorists and the Nations Supporting Them," Office of Legal Counsel, U.S. Department of Justice, September 25, 2001, www.usdoj.gov/olc/warpowers 925.htm (accessed December 14, 2007); and Bradford Berenson, "Examining Proposals to Limit Guantanamo Detainees' Access to Habeas Corpus Review," Testimony to the United States Senate Committee on the Judiciary, September 25, 2006, http://judiciary.senate.gov/testimony .cfm?id=2416&wit_id=5775 (accessed September 29, 2006). On the *Hamdan* case, see "Hamdan v. Rumsfeld, Secretary of Defense, et al.— Certiorari to the United States Court of Appeals for the District of Columbia Circuit," argued March 28, 2006—decided June 29, 2006, No. 05-184. http://caselaw.lp.findlaw.com/scripts/getcase.pl?court=US&vol 1=000&invol=05184&friend=nytimes (accessed March 21, 2008). Note that *Hamdan* and *Hamdi* are two entirely different cases.

3. It is as if these sites were declared "res nullis" and not subject to the customs of civil society. The Supreme Court has not ruled on the claim of the nonsovereignty of Guantanamo, restricting its judgments—as in *Hamdan v. Rumsfeld*—to procedural questions. Congress, in turn, has legalized dubious procedures without challenging the foundational claim regarding sovereignty. See, e.g., Kaplan, "Where Is Guantánamo?" As explained in a review of a recent book by Michael Ratner and Ellen Ray, "Under the terms of the Platt Agreement, the [Guantanamo] lease can only be terminated by 'mutual assent.' Thus, although Cuba has not agreed to the lease and has not accepted rent payments since 1959, the United States retains the lease because it chooses to do so. Second, the lease contains a provision that gives the United States 'complete jurisdiction and control over the territory,' but 'recognizes the continuance of the ultimate sovereignty of the Republic of Cuba.' This provision lies at the heart of the U.S. Supreme Court decisions that have applied unique standards in assessing the actions of the U.S. government with respect to Guantanamo detainees. In the arguments that were pending before the Supreme Court at the time of the book's publication, the U.S. government invoked these clauses to argue that U.S. courts lack jurisdiction over Guantanamo detainees because Guantanamo is under the sovereignty of Cuba, but that Cuba has no authority as to what goes on in Guantanamo because the United States has complete jurisdiction over it." Rebecca J. Hamilton, Review of Michael Ratner and Ellen Ray, *Guantánamo: What The World Should Know* (White River, Vt.: Chelsea Green Publishing, 2004), in *Harvard Human Rights Journal* 18 (Spring 2005), www.law.harvard .edu/students/orgs/hrj/iss18/booknotes-Guant_aa.shtml (accessed December 17, 2007). See also Joseph Lazar, "International Legal Status of Guantanamo Bay," *American Journal of International Law* 62, 3 (July 1968): 730–740; and Gary L. Maris, "Guantanamo: No Rights of Occupancy," *American Journal of International Law* 63, 1 (January 1969): 114–116.

4. I use "executive branch" here in lieu of the executive or president, in recognition that it is a collective, if not always coherent, actor that constitutes the core of Imperium; see Louis Fisher, "The 'Sole Organ' Doctrine," *The Law Library of Congress*, August 2006 (2006-03236), www.fas.org/sgp/eprint/fisher.pdf (accessed September 26, 2007); Frederick A. O. Schwartz Jr. and Aziz Z. Huq, *Unchecked and Unbalanced—Presidential Power in a Time of Terror* (New York: The New Press, 2007); Jack L. Goldsmith, *The Terror Presidency—Law and Judgment Inside the Bush Administration* (New York: Norton, 2007); and Jeffrey Rosen, "Conscience of a Conservative," *New York Times Sunday Maga-*

zine, September 9, 2007, www.nytimes.com/2007/09/09/magazine /09rosen.html? (accessed September 9, 2007).

5. See Clinton Rossiter, *Constitutional Dictatorship—Crisis Government in the Modern Democracies* (Princeton, N.J.: Princeton University Press, 1948); Clinton L. Rossiter, "Constitutional Dictatorship in the Atomic Age," *The Review of Politics* 11, 4 (October 1949): 395–418. On the morality of nuclear weapons and war as seen in the 1980s, see James Child, *Nuclear War: The Moral Dimension* (New Brunswick, N.J.: Transaction Books, 1986); and Avner Cohen and Stephen Lee, eds., *Nuclear Weapons and the Future of Humanity* (Totowa, N.J.: Rowman & Allanheld, 1986).

6. See Scott Shane, "C.I.A. Agents Sense Shifting Support for Methods," *New York Times*, December 13, 2007, www.nytimes. com/2007/12/13/washington/13inquire.html (accessed December 13, 2007); and Mark Danner, *Torture and Truth—America, Abu Ghraib, and the War on Terror* (New York: New York Review of Books, 2004).

7. Ronnie D. Lipschutz, with James K. Rowe, *Globalization, Governmentality and Global Politics—Regulation for the Rest of Us?* (London: Routledge, 2005); Philip Bobbitt, *The Shield of Achilles—War, Peace, and the Course of History* (New York: Knopf, 2002). The Supreme Court's March 2008 hearing of a challenge to the District of Columbia's gun control law illustrates the Talmudic extremes to which such interpretation can go. See Tony Mauro, "Supreme Court Hears Arguments in D.C. Gun Ban Case," *Legal Times*, March 18, 2008, http://www.law .com/jsp/article.jsp?id=1205848854160 (accessed March 21, 2008).

8. Michael Stokes Paulsen, "How to Interpret the Constitution (and How Not To)," *The Yale Law Journal* 115 (2006): 2036–2066, www.yalelawjournal.org/pdf/115–8/Paulsen.pdf (accessed December 17, 2007); and Judith Pryor, "Unwritten Constitutions?" *European Journal of English Studies* 11, 1 (2007): 79–92.

9. See, e.g., Kalypso Nicolaidis, "The Struggle for Europe," *Dissent* (Fall 2005): 11–17, http://users.ox.ac.uk/~ssfc0041/struggleEUrope .pdf (accessed December 17, 2007).

10. Thus, as in *Hamdan v. Rumsfeld* and other cases, individuals stand in for governments. The problem of indicting institutions for structural violence and violations is addressed in Johann Galtung, *Human Rights in Another Key* (Cambridge: Polity, 1995). See also Elizabeth Borgwardt, *A New Deal for the World: America's Vision for Human Rights* (Cambridge, Mass.: Belknap Press of Harvard University Press, 2005).

11. On consumer citizenship, see Stephen Gill, "The Global Panopticon? The Neoliberal State, Economic Life, and Democratic

Surveillance," *Alternatives* 2, 1 (January–March 1995): 1–50; Michelle Everson, "Legal Constructions of the Consumer" (paper presented at a conference on "Knowing Consumers: Actors, Images, Identities in Modern History," at the Zentrum für Interdisziplinäre Forschung in Bielefeld, Germany, February 26–28, 2004), www.consume.bbk .ac.uk/ZIF%20Conference/Everson.doc (accessed December 17, 2007); and Michelle Everson and Christian Joerges, "Consumer Citizenship in Postnational Constellations?" European University Institute, Department of Law, Law No. 2006/47, http://cadmus.eui.eu/dspace/ bitstream/1814/6547/1/LAW%202006–47.pdf (accessed December 17, 2007). On cosmopolitan citizenship, see David Chandler, "New Rights for Old? Cosmopolitan Citizenship and the Critique of State Sovereignty," *Political Studies* 51, 2 (2003): 332–349, www.blackwell synergy.com/doi/pdf/10.1111/1467–9248.00427 (accessed December 17, 2007); and Gerard Delanty, "Cosmopolitan Citizenship," in *Public Sociologies Reader,* ed. Judith R. Blau and Keri E. Iyall Smith, 37–50 (Lanham, Md.: Rowman & Littlefield, 2006).

12. As noted previously, many putative terrorists are being taken into custody in lawful and governed spaces, such as Britain, Germany, and Denmark; see, e.g., Eric Geiger, "Germany Sees Alarming Threat from Citizens Who Convert to Islam," *San Francisco Chronicle*, September 7, 2007, www.sfgate.com/cgi-bin/article.cgi?file=/c/a/2007/09/ /07/MN0LRP6S4.DTL (accessed September 7, 2007); Monstersand critics.com, "Germans Watch Rising Conversion to Islam with Concern," September 6, 2007, http://news.monstersandcritics.com/europe /news/article_1352428.php/SIDEBAR_Germans_watch_rising_ conversion_to_Islam_with_concern (accessed September 15, 2007); and Regina Kerner, "Unter Beobachtung Nach den Festnahmen im Sauerland wird die Frage debattiert, ob zum Islam übergetretene Deutsche besonders anfällig sind für Radikalismus," *Berliner Zeitung,* September 6, 2007, www.berlinonline.de/berliner-zeitung/print/tages thema/683848.html (accessed September 15, 2007). On the caliphate, see Eli Lake, "Victory Will Come as in Cold War, Rumsfeld Predicts," *New York Sun,* November 19, 2007, www.nysun.com/article/66643 (accessed December 17, 2007).

13. On Schmitt, see *Political Theology: Four Chapters on the Concept of Sovereignty* (Cambridge, Mass: MIT Press, 1965); on Kelsen, see, e.g., Iain Steward, "The Critical Legal Science of Hans Kelsen," *Journal of Law and Society* 17, 3 (Autumn, 1990): 273–308.

14. See Ellen Yaroshefsky, "Secret Evidence Is Slowly Eroding the Adversary System: CIPA and FISA in the Courts," *Hofstra Law Review* 34 (2006): 1063–1092.

15. Charlie Savage, "Bush Challenges Hundreds of Laws," *Boston Globe*, April 30, 2006, www.boston.com/news/nation/articles/2006/04/30/bush_challenges_hundreds_of_laws/ (accessed August 13, 2007).

16. The War Powers Act of 1973, Public Law 93-148, 93rd Congress, 1st sess. (November 7, 1973) was intended to impose limits on the executive branch with respect to the waging of war without authorization of Congress. For the most part, it has proved ineffective and its constitutionality has never been judged by the U.S. Supreme Court. For a conservative discussion of presidential war powers, see Curtis A. Bradley and Jack L. Goldsmith, "Congressional Authorization and the War on Terrorism," *Harvard Law Review* 118, 7 (May 2005): 2048–2133, www.harvardlawreview.org/issues/118/May05/Bradley_Goldsmith01FTX.pdf (accessed December 10, 2007).

17. Felicia Lee, "Constitutionally, A Risky Business," *New York Times*, May 31, 2003, http://query.nytimes.com/gst/fullpage.html?res=9F05E2DF1730F932A05756C0A9659C8B63 (accessed December 15, 2007).

18. Nicholas J. Wheeler, "The Humanitarian Responsibilities of Sovereignty: Explaining the Development of a New Norm of Military Intervention for Humanitarian Purposes in International Society," in *Humanitarian Intervention and International Relations*, ed. Jennifer M. Walsh, 29–51 (Oxford: Oxford University Press, 2003).

19. The White House, *The National Security Strategy of the United States*, September 2002, p. iv.

20. During discussions about whether the Foreign Intelligence Surveillance Act might affect the wiretapping of international calls "involving terrorists," Cheney's counsel, David Addington, is reported to have said, "We're one bomb away from getting rid of that obnoxious [FISA] court." Cited in Rosen, "Conscience of a Conservative." Even a Congress controlled by Democrats has proven itself unwilling to consider impeachment of President Bush for what are, quite demonstrably, unconstitutional actions.

21. George W. Bush, "Press Conference by the President," The White House Office of the Press Secretary, August 18, 2006, www.whitehouse.gov/news/releases/2006/08/20060821.html (accessed November 29, 2007). On the public's belief, see Angus Reid Global Monitor, "Half of Americans Link Hussein and al-Qaeda," January 7, 2007, www.angus-reid.com/polls/view/14319 (accessed March 21, 2008). On the absence of any link between Iraq and 9/11, see Kevin M. Woods with James Lacey, *Iraqi Perspectives Project—Saddam and Terrorism: Emerging Insights from Captured Iraqi Documents,* IDA Paper P-4151,

Vol. 1 (Alexandria, Va.: Institute for Defense Analysis Joint Advanced Warfighting Program, redacted November 2007), http://a.abcnews.com/images/pdf/Pentagon_Report_V1.pdf (accessed March 21, 2008).

Chapter 8

1. On the state of the U.S. occupation of Iraq, see John J. Kruzel, "U.S. Ambassador Presents Iraq Progress Report to Congress," American Forces Press Service, September 10, 2007, and linked articles, www.defenselink.mil/news/newsarticle.aspx?id=47387 (accessed December 19, 2007). On the status of the GWOT, see "President Bush Discusses Global War on Terror," The White House, November 1, 2007, www.whitehouse.gov/news/releases/2007/11/20071101-4.html (accessed December 19, 2007). On assessments of the global economy, see "Are We in a Recession?" *New York Times*, December 16, 2007, www.nytimes.com/2007/12/16/opinion/16recession.html?ref=opinion (accessed December 16, 2007) and citations in chapter 6 of this book. On mea culpas, see Michael Ignatieff, "Getting Iraq Wrong," *New York Times*, August 5, 2007, www.nytimes.com/2007/08/05/magazine/05iraq-t.html (accessed August 10, 2007).

2. I do not explore this point further here, but see Robert Boyer and Yves Saillard, eds., *Régulation Theory: The State of the Art* (London: Routledge, 2002); Robert Boyer and Daniel Drache, eds., *States against Markets: The Limits of Globalization* (London: Routledge, 1996); and Daniel Drache, ed., *The Market Or the Public Domain? Global Governance and the Asymmetry of Power* (London: Routledge, 2001). See also Philip G. Cerny, "Structuring the Political Arena: Public Goods, States and Governance in a Globalizing World," in *Global Political Economy: Contemporary Theories,* ed. Ronen Palan, 21–35 (London: Routledge, 2000); Bob Jessop, "Capitalism, Steering and the State" (paper posted to the Web site of the Alexander Von Humboldt Lectures, Radboud University of Nijmegen, Netherlands, 2004), www.ru.nl/socgeo/colloquium/CapitalismSteeringState.pdf (accessed December 15, 2007); and Shelley Hurt, "Science, Power, and the State: U.S. Foreign Policy, Intellectual Property Law, and the Origins of the World Trade Organization, 1969–1994" (PhD diss., Department of Political Science, The New School for Social Research, 2008).

3. Michael Hardt and Antonio Negri, *Empire* (Cambridge, Mass.: Harvard University Press, 2000); and *Multitude—War and Democracy in*

the Age of Empire (New York: Penguin, 2004). On property rights, see J. G. A. Pocock, *Virtue, Commerce, and History: Essays on Political Thought and History* (Cambridge, England: Cambridge University Press, 1985), chs. 3, 6; and Peter Drahos with John Braithwaite, *Information Feudalism—Who Owns the Knowledge Economy* (London: Earthscan, 2002).

4. Recognizing, of course, that such arrangements are unlikely to be wholly equitable and fair. Cooperation usually involves elements of coercion, discipline, and advantage. On the notion of a world state, see Alex Wendt, "Why a World State Is Inevitable," *European Journal of International Affairs* 9, 4 (2003):491–542. On the naturalization of anarchy, see Bobbitt, *The Shield of Achilles*. On the moderation of anarchy, see Hedley Bull, *The Anarchical Society,* 3rd ed. (New York: Columbia University Press, 2002); and Barry Buzan, *People, States, and Fear: An Agenda for International Security Studies in the Post–Cold War Era,* 2nd ed. (Boulder, Colo.: Lynne Rienner, 1991).

5. On rules and rule, see Nicholas G. Onuf, *World of Our Making: Rules and Rule in Social Theory and International Relations* (Columbia: University of South Carolina Press, 1989). On systemic imperatives, see Robert Jervis, "The Compulsive Empire," *Foreign Policy* 137 (July/August 2003): 82–87. On the Wolfowitz plan, see Patrick E. Tyler, "U.S. Strategy Plan Calls for Insuring No Rivals Develop," *New York Times,* March 8, 1992, http://query.nytimes.com/gst/fullpage.html ?res=9E0CE5D61E38F93BA35750C0A964958260 (accessed December 19, 2007); and Patrick E. Tyler, "Pentagon Imagines New Enemies to Fight in Post-Cold-War Era," *New York Times,* February 17, 1992, http://query.nytimes.com/gst/fullpage.html?res=9E0CE5D61F39F93 4A25751C0A964958260 (accessed December 19, 2007).

6. "Rebuilding America's Defenses—Strategy, Forces and Resources for a New Century," Project for the New American Century, 2000, p. i, www.newamericancentury.org/RebuildingAmericas Defenses.pdf (accessed December 17, 2007). The 2006 *National Security Strategy* did not reject its predecessor, but in many ways was more modest in its tone, claims, and objectives.

7. Some insights into the social composition of "global governance" can be found by consulting "Global Governance and Public Accountability," *Government and Opposition* 39, 2 (2004), www.black well-synergy.com/toc/goop/39/2 (accessed December 15, 2007).

8. That such a "right" is already claimed by the United States and Russia is recognized in the international law literature, although not with broad approval. On the "right" of intervention, see Helen Dexter, "New War, Good War and the War on Terror: Explaining, Excusing and Creating Western Neo-interventionism," *Development and Change* 38, 6

(2007): 1055–1071; and Nicholas J. Wheeler, "The Humanitarian Responsibilities of Sovereignty: Explaining the Development of a New Norm of Military Intervention for Humanitarian Purposes in International Society," in *Humanitarian Intervention and International Relations*, ed. Jennifer M. Walsh, 29–51 (Oxford: Oxford University Press, 2003).

9. Fred L. Block, *The Origins of International Economic Disorder* (Berkeley: University of California Press, 1977).

10. On the origins of the Cold War economy, see Robert A. Pollard, *Economic Security and the Origins of the Cold War, 1945–1950* (New York: Columbia University Press, 1985); and Beverly Crawford, *Economic Vulnerability in International Relations* (New York: Columbia University Press, 1993).

11. Andrew Bacevich, *The New American Militarism: How Americans Are Seduced by War* (Oxford: Oxford University Press, 2005).

12. The purchase of major chunks of American financial institutions, such as CitiGroup, by the sovereign investment funds of Abu Dhabi and Singapore suggests the beginning of such a rescue; see CNNMoney.com, "Dubai Denies Citi Funding Rumor," March 6, 2008, http://money.cnn.com/2008/03/06/news/companies/dubai_citigroup.ap/index.htm?section=money_news_international (accessed March 21, 2008).

13. On intellectual property, see Drahos, *Information Feudalism*. On enclosure of the commons, see James Boyle, "The Second Enclosure Movement and the Construction of the Public Domain," *Law and Contemporary Problems*, 66 (Winter/Spring 2003): 33–74.

14. This is not to ignore the upper tier's obvious interest in police power which, to a growing degree, blends seamlessly into military power, and vice versa. Hardt and Negri address this point in *Multitude*.

15. The quote is from *Multitude*, p. 347.

16. Sandra Halperin, *War and Social Change in Modern Europe* (Cambridge, England: Cambridge University Press, 2004), 54, 53.

17. On secret societies, see Reinhart Koselleck, *Critique and Crisis—Enlightenment and the Pathogenesis of Modern Society* (Cambridge, Mass.: MIT Press, 1988).

INDEX

ABOUT THE AUTHOR

Ronnie D. Lipschutz is professor of politics and codirector of the Center for Global, International, and Regional Studies at the University of California–Santa Cruz. His primary areas of research, writing, and teaching include international politics, global environmental affairs, U.S. foreign policy, empire and religion, globalization, international regulation, technology and public policy, and film, fiction, and politics.